W9-BJO-610

SOUTH AFRICA

BY
MIKE CADMAN

D0123817

Produced by
Thomas Cook Publishing

Written by Mike Cadman

Original photography by Mike Cadman and Trevor Samson

Original design by Laburnum Technologies PVT Ltd

Cover design by Liz Lyon Design, Oxford

Editing and page layout by Jacana Media
PO Box 2004, Houghton, 2041, South Africa

Published by Thomas Cook Publishing
A division of Thomas Cook Tour Operations Limited
PO Box 227, The Thomas Cook Business Park, Units 15–16,
Coningsby Road, Peterborough PE3 8SB, United Kingdom
E-mail: books@thomascook.com
www.thomascookpublishing.com

ISBN: 1-841574-29-5

Text © 2005 Thomas Cook Publishing
Maps © 2005 Thomas Cook Publishing
First edition © 2005 Thomas Cook Publishing

Head of Thomas Cook Publishing: Chris Young
Project Editor: Charlotte Christensen
Project Administrator: Michelle Warrington
Production/DTP: Steven Collins

Although every care has been taken in compiling this publication, and the contents are believed to be correct at the time of printing, Thomas Cook Tour Operations Limited cannot accept any responsibility for errors or omissions, however caused, or for changes in details given in the guidebook, or for the consequences of any reliance on the information provided.

The opinions and assessments expressed in this book do not necessarily represent those of Thomas Cook Tour Operations Limited.

Printed and bound in Spain by: Grafo Industrias Gráficas, Basauri

Front cover credits: left © Dynamic Graphics Group/IT Stock Free/Alamy; centre © SCPhotos/Alamy; right © Travel Ink/Alamy. Back cover credits: left © Hugh Sitton/Alamy; right © Chris Fredriksson/Alamy.

C o n t e n t s

Introduction

Table Mountain stands tall over Cape Town with its fashionable beaches and productive winelands. Almost 2,000km (1,600 miles) to the north-east, the equally famous Kruger National Park shelters South Africa's largest population of elephants, lions and other creatures that thrive in the vast expanse of hot, wild bush. In between, lies most of South Africa, a nation of more than 44 million people with a rich and complex social fabric, 11 official languages, a zest for sport, and a landscape that boasts remarkable geographic splendour and variability.

Sugarbush protea, Helderberg, Western Cape

In KwaZulu-Natal, crystal-clear streams drain from the sometimes snow-capped uKhahlamba-Drakensberg mountains, while in the Northern Cape cheetahs and martial eagles search for prey in the rolling grass-covered sand dunes and desert scrub of the Kgalagadi Transfrontier Park. Along the country's west coast the icy Benguela current makes swimming a pastime only for the brave, but conversely Africa's southernmost coral reefs occur in the warm waters along the north-east coast.

These and other geographic and climatic contrasts contribute to making South Africa's flora and fauna amongst the most diverse of any region of comparable size anywhere.

In the middle of the country the teeming metropolis of Johannesburg and its neighbouring towns and cities attract visitors and work-seekers from all over the country, and even from neighbouring states.

South Africa is the economic powerhouse of Africa, and although many citizens are poor, the country has an extensive and well-maintained road system, efficient air links and good tourism infrastructure. The mining industry and rich deposits of gold, diamonds, platinum and other minerals have long been the mainstay of the economy. There is, however, an increasing focus on the technology, manufacturing and tourism sectors.

In some fields the constraints of apartheid are being shed relatively quickly, and today business leaders,

Copyright: South African Tourism
The popular Durban beachfront, KwaZulu-Natal

politicians, academics and sportsmen and women come from all segments of the country's diverse population. In other aspects the transition from apartheid has not been as easy, but more and more children, known locally as the 'born frees', have no memory of South Africa without democracy, a concept which arrived with the 1994 election won by Nelson Mandela and his African National Congress party.

South Africa's youth, in keeping with global trends, are part of a rapidly urbanising population, and many people live in informal settlements around cities and towns.

South Africa's cities are not old by European standards – Cape Town, the country's oldest city, was open countryside in 1652, and Johannesburg is only 120 years old – but fossil evidence reveals an ancient history of human habitation. Some of the oldest hominid fossils on record have been found near Johannesburg, and archaeologists can trace fairly constant human habitation of the region for hundreds of thousands of years.

In recent history, migrants from many parts of Africa and Europe have made the country their home, but whatever their ancestry, many South Africans' lives incorporate aspects of other cultures as a matter of daily routine. Cuisine, fashion and the arts all increasingly reflect this amalgam of traditions.

Al fresco dining in Franschhoek, Western Cape

Geography and Climate

South Africa covers some 1,2 million sq km which is more than twice the size of France or a bit bigger than the US states of California and Texas combined. It lies roughly between 22 and 35 degrees south of the equator, and has 2,950km (1,829 miles) of coastline washed by the Atlantic Ocean in the west and the Indian Ocean in the east.

Pakamisa Game Reserve, Northern KwaZulu-Natal

South Africa shares borders with Namibia, Botswana, Zimbabwe, Mozambique, Swaziland and Lesotho. The latter is entirely surrounded by South Africa.

The climate varies markedly, with most of the country experiencing the greater part of its rainfall in summer. On the Highveld (literally 'the high land'), and in the uKhahlamba-

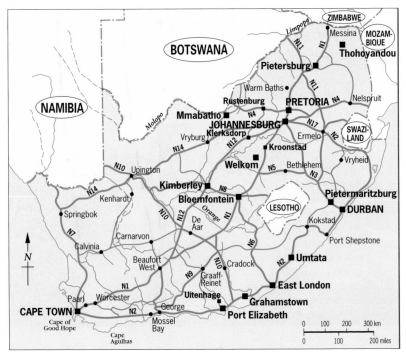

Drakensberg mountains, dramatic thunderstorms sweep across the countryside on summer afternoons often disappearing over the horizon and leaving clear rain-scrubbed skies.

The Western Cape has a Mediterranean climate and experiences warm to hot dry summers and cool, wet winters.

Temperatures in the interior sometimes climb to over 36°C (97°F) in summer, but in winter can plummet to well below 0°C (32°F) at night in the various mountain ranges and in the deserts. Deserts are not always hot, and although the Kalahari Desert regularly experiences daytime temperatures well over 40°C (104°F), night-time winter temperatures can drop as low as –10°C (18°F).

Most of South Africa lies on a plateau fringed by a coastal belt of varying width, and many of the basic geographic and climatic features spread across one or two, and in some cases several, provincial boundaries. The 2,300km (1,426 miles) Orange River for example, South Africa's longest river, rises in Lesotho and then flows along the borders of the Free State and Eastern Cape. It then heads through the Northern Cape to enter the Atlantic, where the borders of South Africa and Namibia meet.

A basic description of the geography and vegetation of each province is listed on *pages 8–9*. South Africa is comprised of nine provinces: Eastern Cape, Free State, Gauteng, KwaZulu-Natal, Limpopo, Mpumalanga, Northern Cape, North West and Western Cape.

Eastern Cape
Long, wide, sandy beaches characterise

Jeffrey's Bay, a favourite surfing spot in the Eastern Cape

much of the Eastern Cape coast, although in the south, high forested ridges run right down to the sea providing spectacular views from cliffs above the waves. Further north the rugged Wild Coast, a region of sea cliffs, deep river valleys and largely empty beaches begins. Not far inland, high fold-mountains that sometimes receive snowfalls roll into the low scrub semi-deserts of the Karoo *(see Eastern Cape on pp34–43).*

Free State

The Free State is primarily open grassland, which begins to dissipate into the semi-deserts of the Karoo and Kalahari in the west. In the east, high ridges with sandstone cliffs form deep valleys, and in winter heavy snowfalls sometimes occur *(see Free State on pp44–45).*

Gauteng

Gauteng is generally a region of open

Boats in the yacht basin,
Durban harbour

grassland-covered plains ribbed with low ridges and the steeper Magaliesberg to the north. Much of the province is more than 1,500m (4,850ft) above sea level *(see Gauteng on pp48–61).*

KwaZulu-Natal (KZN)

The 3,200m (10,000ft) high uKhahlamba-Drakensberg mountains form the western boundary of this province. South Africa's highest point, Mafadi, 3,446m (10,449ft), is in the Injisuthi region of these mountains. The land falls away rapidly to the east in a jumble of rolling hills, which run down to the sub-tropical coast. The south coast has many rocky coves, but the beaches become sandier along the north coast *(see KwaZulu-Natal on pp62– 83).*

Limpopo

Three major mountain ranges, the Waterberg, the Soutpansberg and the Northern Drakensberg cut through this province, which is primarily open bushveld (grassland savannah interspersed with thorn trees). The Drakensberg form the edge of the escarpment, which drops steeply to the Lowveld (low country). The Lowveld comprises many vegetation forms, but in simple terms is dominated by bushveld and mopane woodlands, which together cover much of the Kruger National Park. Summers are very hot and winters mild. *(see Limpopo on pp84–5).*

Mpumalanga

High-altitude open grasslands in the west, south and south-east of this province drop to the Lowveld down northern Drakenberg passes similarly steep to those in Limpopo Province. This is an important farming province, and also includes the southern half of the Kruger National Park *(see Mpumalanga on pp86–95).*

Northern Cape

The Northern Cape falls into the Karoo and Kalahari semi-desert zones. Much of the Karoo is covered with shrubs and sparse grasslands, and is an important cattle and sheep-farming region. Camel thorn trees, grasses specially adapted to the dry conditions and huge skies are the trademarks of the Kalahari. In the south-west the harsh Namaqualand region usually bursts into colour once a year as millions of flowers bloom after winter rains *(see Northern Cape on pp98–103).*

North West

Much of this province is covered by open bushveld, and the Waterberg mountains act as an important watershed. In the centre of the province, the ancient Pilanesberg volcano makes a dramatic setting for the well-run Pilanesberg National Park. The west gives way to the arid Kalahari *(see North West on pp96–7).*

Western Cape

Although the west coast is cool and sparsely vegetated, the rest of this province's coastline is a mix of secluded coves, broad sandy beaches, and mountains that plunge directly into the ocean, breakers crashing at their feet. Inland, a maze of fold-mountains finally gives way to the plains of the Karoo. Many of the famed Cape winelands shelter on the slopes and in the valleys formed by these mountains *(see Western Cape on pp106–21).*

Hout Bay at night, Western Cape

History

100,000 BC	Archaeological evidence shows southern Africa is already inhabited by *Homo sapiens*.
8,000 BC	San hunters inhabit parts of South Africa.
AD 1–1500	Iron-working spreads through central and southern Africa as Bantu people begin to move southwards and dominate the San and Khoikhoi peoples.
1488	Bartholomeu Dias rounds the Cape and reaches Mossel Bay.
1497	Vasco da Gama rounds the Cape and charts the sea route to India.
1652	Arrival of Jan van Riebeeck, first commander of the Dutch East India Company's Cape settlement.
1688	French Huguenots arrive.
1779	First of nine settler-Xhosa frontier wars in the Eastern Cape.
1795	First British occupation of the Cape.

Slave bells, Stellenbosch

1806	Second British occupation of the Cape.
1820	Large group of British settlers arrive in the Grahamstown area.
mid-1830s	The Great Trek into the interior begins as Boers grow resentful of British rule in the Cape colony.
1838	Battle of Blood River: a small force of Voortrekkers defeats the Zulu.
1850s	Independent Boer republics of Orange Free State and Transvaal are established.
1867	Discovery of diamonds near Kimberley – the diamond rush begins.
1879	Battles of Isandhlwana and Rorke's Drift.

1880	First Anglo-Boer War (won by the Boers).
1886	Gold discovered. Johannesburg founded.
1899–1902	South African War (formerly the Anglo-Boer War – won by the British).
1910	Union of South Africa.
1912	The African National Congress is formed.
1913	The Natives Land Act reserves most land for the use of White people.
1948	Victory for the National Party in white elections.
1950	Various apartheid legislation introduced and tightened during the next few years.
1952	The ANC's defiance campaign begins.
1958	Dr Hendrik Verwoerd becomes prime minister. Apartheid strictly enforced.
1960	Referendum for South African independence. Sharpeville Massacre: demonstrators against the Pass Laws are fired on (69 killed, 180 injured). State bans ANC.
1961	South Africa leaves the Commonwealth and becomes a republic. The ANC begins its armed struggle. ANC leader *Nkosi* (Chief) Albert Luthuli wins Nobel Peace Prize.
1964	Rivonia Treason Trial: Nelson Mandela and seven other ANC members are sentenced to life imprisonment. South Africa excluded from Olympic Games.

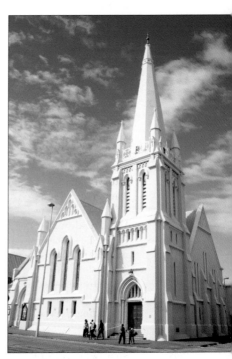

Trinity Methodist Church, East London

1966	Verwoerd assassinated by parliamentary messenger.
1967	Professor Chris Barnard performs the world's first heart transplant.
1975	South Africa invades Angola.
1976	Police open fire on student protestors in Soweto on 16 June. The shootings lead to nationwide rioting, resulting in hundreds of deaths.
1977	Mandatory UN arms embargo. Steve Biko dies in detention.
1983	A new constitution allows three separate houses in parliament – for Whites, Coloureds and Indians.
1984	Archbishop Desmond Tutu wins the Nobel Peace Prize.
1985	ANC President Oliver Tambo, Rev. Jesse Jackson and Archbishop Huddleston head a 100,000-strong march through London demanding sanctions. State of Emergency declared in sections of the country. Political violence sweeps townships.
1985–86	Thousands of people are detained without trial during continued State of Emergency. Violence continues intermittently for next five years.
1989	F W de Klerk becomes president succeeding P W Botha.
1990	Nelson Mandela released from prison. The ANC and other banned political organisations are legalised. National Party

A 19th century carriage at the Calgary Transport Museum, Eastern Cape

government abandons apartheid, and begins negotiations to end it. The ANC suspends the armed struggle.

1992	Whites-only referendum leads to a 69 per cent vote to continue reforms.
1993	Nelson Mandela and President F W de Klerk share the Nobel Peace Prize.
1994	Democratic elections in April; ANC President Nelson Mandela elected President of South Africa. South Africa re-enters the Commonwealth.
1995	The Truth and Reconciliation Commission under Archbishop Desmond Tutu is appointed to hear evidence of apartheid atrocities.
1999	The second democratic election is held and Mandela steps down as President. The ANC wins and Thabo Mbeki becomes President.
2004	The third democratic election is held and the ANC returns to power. Mbeki remains President.

AIDS

The AIDS epidemic is one of the greatest issues facing South Africa, and has enormous social and economic consequences. Many children have been orphaned after their parents have died from AIDS-related diseases. Many skilled people have been lost to the economy after falling sick and later dying.

The Government was initially very slow to respond to the crisis and, in many cases, the private sector took the lead in education and medication.

Nearly all HIV in South Africa is spread through participating in unprotected sex. Blood transfusions in large hospitals are responsible for very few cases. Private hospitals use world-class technology.

Education is an important tool in the fight against HIV/AIDS

Governance

South Africa in the 21st century is a country hard at work creating an economically viable, functional democracy, but at the same time is intent on enjoying the journey. The excitement and sheer relief of the first-ever democratic election in 1994, the jubilation that greeted the election of Nelson Mandela as President and the realisation that South Africa could hold its head high in the global community of nations is old hat now. The memories, however, of those heady days will always be treasured.

Ex-President
Nelson Mandela

Now the euphoria has transformed into determination, and there is overwhelming consensus among citizens that there is an important task to accomplish. Alleviating poverty and unemployment and improving education and health are all major issues facing the government and the nation, but despite the scale of the task, there is no lack of enthusiasm. Most people accept that addressing these issues properly will be a major step towards helping to reduce the very high crime rate.

For much of the 1980s and early 1990s South Africa's political turmoil made international news headlines, and the name Nelson Mandela became famous all over the world. South Africa's transition to democracy without a full-blown war was hailed as an example of conciliation and common sense. The country has now had two fully democratic elections since 1994 and, although the ruling African National Congress (ANC) is by far the largest party, political debate and argument is vibrant and no more vituperative than in any other democracy.

After years of isolation, South Africa has come to play an important political and economic role in Africa. The country's politicians have contributed significantly toward the slow process of establishing unity on a difficult continent. South African diplomats have helped work towards the resolution of several wars in Africa, and have played

Pretoria skyline

Elections are hotly contested, but there is always time for lunch

an important role in trying to improve trade agreements, foreign debt write-offs, and other issues important to poor nations.

Not all of the government's views, particularly with regard to the policies of some African countries leaders and Middle Eastern politics, have met with the approval of developed nations. South Africa, nevertheless, maintains good relations with many countries' around the globe. This level of international acceptance would have been unthinkable during the 1980s and early 1990s when apartheid was in its death throes.

During the 1980s, the National Party (NP) government clamped down hard on the popular uprising sweeping the Black townships, and tens of thousands of people, including children, were

detained without trial. A series of States of Emergency were declared giving the police and military vast powers. For decades, many political books were banned – it was illegal to quote people like Mandela or even to possess his writings. Nearly all political opposition was outlawed, and the press was severely censored. Thousands of people died in political conflict, many killed by police bullets. The political insurrection was the culmination of many events over many years. Apartheid was the formal policy of denying Black people the vote, the right to free movement, the right to employment and incorporated numerous other legalised injustices. Black people had been denied many rights since European settlers first arrived in Cape Town in 1652.

Resistance against discrimination

manifested itself in many ways over the centuries. It was, however, only after the conservative National Party came to power in 1948 that parties such as the ANC began organised resistance in earnest. The 1960 Sharpeville Massacre, where police shot dead 67 protesters, and the life sentence handed down to Nelson Mandela in 1964 after he was found guilty of treason and sabotage, were just two of the incidents which raised the level of resistance. The state met this with severe oppression.

Thousands of people perceived by the state to be political opponents were jailed and many were tortured. In 1976 the Soweto riots, which were sparked after police opened fire on protesting school children, ignited nationwide unrest. This unrest continued sporadically until after Mandela was released from prison in 1990.

While the state was continually involved in attempting to suppress Black political aspirations, White South Africans enjoyed one of the highest standards of living in the world. This was at considerable cost, however, because international sanctions, sporting, cultural and travel restrictions eventually took their toll. To exacerbate matters, the aggressive NP leadership drew South Africa deeper and deeper into guerrilla wars in neighbouring states, first in Namibia (South West Africa), over which they had been given control by the League of Nations in 1919, and later in Angola.

By the mid-1980s economic sanctions had tightened considerably and this, coupled with the expense of fighting wars in neighbouring states, had a serious impact on the economy. As the Berlin Wall was coming down and many former Soviet States were undergoing their own liberation, the South African government buckled under both internal and international pressure. The government finally made the decision to release Mandela and un-ban political parties.

In 1990 Mandela walked free, and four years later, after prolonged and intense negotiations by representatives of nearly all South Africans, he ushered in a new South Africa to the salute of military helicopters flying the country's new flag and the acclaim of a rapturous nation.

Statue of Cecil John Rhodes in Cape Town

Mounted police patrol past the Houses of Parliament in Cape Town

Culture

South Africa's cultural heritage reflects the country's complex history, and African, European and Asian influences all thread their way through the art, music and literature of the region. South Africa's relatively recent transition to democracy has led to a significant shift towards exploring and embracing Africa's rich cultural background, and this heritage is actively being promoted with a greater sense of pride than at any other time in history.

Colourful detail outside the National Gallery

Art

South Africa's oldest art form *(see box on p22)* is the rock art and engravings of the San (Bushmen). However, the 17th, 18th and 19th centuries saw the development of a school of European artists intent on creating a record of the landscapes, people and animals in what was to them a strange new country.

Perhaps the best known of these painters were Thomas Baines and Thomas Bowler whose work created an accurate, if somewhat stylised, record of the country as it then was.

Western influence continued to dominate until well into the 20th century, but artists such as Walter Battiss slowly gave painting a more South African flavour.

Black artists including George Pemba and Gerard Sekoto, although almost unknown in South Africa at the time,

African beadwork at a flea market

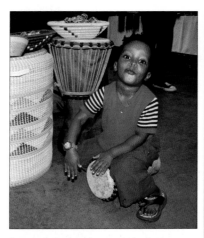

A youngster makes his own music at a flea market

took this trend to a new level in the 1940s, and today their work fetches high prices. Later in the 20th century, many artists began using their work as a form of protest against apartheid. Modern South African art draws on many influences, and increasing numbers of young South Africans are focusing on more traditional African styles. Many art galleries and markets also sell traditional African day-to-day items including bowls, sleeping mats and symbolic beadwork as art.

Music

Whether the music is played on a cowhide drum, a *marimba* (a form of xylophone usually made from a gourd), a Stradivarius violin or an electric guitar, someone in South Africa will consider the entertainment 'traditional'. As with so many other aspects of the country, local music has its roots in many cultures and traditions, and is continually evolving according to new demands and trends. Western and African influences mix easily, and radio stations and music stores offer everything from *kwaito* (a form of rap), reggae, jazz, blues, classical and hard rock to general pop. Jazz trumpeter Hugh Masekela and singer Miriam Makeba have been known internationally since the 1960s, and younger artists such as Yvonne Chaka Chaka with her cross-cultural rhythms have built followings across Africa. The piano work of Abdullah Ibrahim (formerly Dollar Brand) has reached almost cult status in some quarters.

Johnny Clegg and his bands Juluka and Savuka pioneered a mix of traditional Zulu music and modern soft rock, and the Soweto String Quartet have managed to combine a mix of classical, jazz and African music into a huge popular product. Music is important to many South Africans, and the focal point of many a tavern or restaurant is the radio or hi-fi.

In rural areas homemade instruments are common, and they are often ingeniously created from items designed for anything but making music. Lengths of fishing line, seeds from trees and disused motor-oil cans are adapted for use in guitars, rattles and drums.

Architecture

South African architecture is a bewildering mix of old, new, rural and modernist, with a huge dose of practicality thrown in for good measure. Older cities are a mix of glass and steel modernist structures, dull and conservative 1960s office blocks

Burgerhuis, Stellenbosch, a fine example of 18th century Cape Dutch architecture

and the occasional Art Deco or Victorian building.

Sandton, near Johannesburg, has been developed over the past 25 years, and is the largest conglomeration of new buildings in the country, with an unusual mix of avant-garde constructions, pseudo-European plazas and even buildings ostentatiously decorated with Roman-style pillars and facades.

Many of the Victorian buildings are found in Pietermaritzburg, Durban and Cape Town, but many smaller towns such as Oudtshoorn contain good examples of this style, a legacy of British colonisation. Perhaps the most well-known form of South African architecture is the Cape Dutch style, which is best displayed in Cape Town itself and the nearby winemaking towns of Stellenbosch, Franschhoek, Paarl and Tulbagh. Thatched-roof buildings with decorative gables and white walls preside over rows of vines. Most have large, ornate double doors and square windows with carefully tended wooden frames.

The Union Buildings – built by Sir Herbert Baker in 1912 – are, arguably, the most easily recognised architectural landmarks in the country. The ornate buildings, decorated with stone pillars and friezes, are still used as the seat of government.

Residential architecture ranges from the opulent – built in whatever style the owner can afford – to the tiny, almost square 'matchbox' houses built as housing for Black people in the formerly racially segregated townships. In poor informal settlements, shacks are often made of corrugated-iron sheeting, wooden-crate panels and even plastic – they may not qualify as architectural masterpieces, but they are home to millions of people. In rural areas, traditional Xhosa, Zulu or Venda huts are still used, but many have been adapted over the years. Zulu 'beehive' huts were made with grass thatched over a wooden frame, although traditional Xhosa and Venda homes tended to have mud walls.

Literature

Although most South African literature is written in English or Afrikaans, the country's writers have explored a wide range of themes and social issues, and their works largely trace the development of modern South Africa. Many writers have achieved international recognition, and the Nobel Prize for Literature was awarded to two South Africans in recent years. Nadine Gordimer (1991) and J M Coetzee (2003), although very different in style, both examine the psychology of apartheid and post-apartheid South Africa. The theme has been consistent among many writers, and the classics *Cry, the Beloved Country* by Alan Paton (1948), *Down Second Avenue* by Es'kia Mphahlele (1959) and *Country of my Skull* by Antjie Krog (1998) dig deeply into the country's collective psyche.

The Pierneef Museum, Graaff Reinet, Eastern Cape

South African poetry covers a very broad range of subjects, ranging from the South African War (Anglo-Boer War), through to a celebration of nature, love and the freedom struggle. Poets, including Sipho Sepamala and Mafika Gwala, used their work to try to raise political awareness when other forms of political expression were outlawed. South Africa has also produced many writers of popular fiction – Wilbur Smith is one of the best-selling authors of all time. Although not literature in the classic sense, South Africa has a very strong publishing industry based on the environment and wildlife. A huge variety of high-quality coffee table books, field guides and popular science works are available at good bookstores.

Drama

Many South African playwrights and actors have achieved international fame. Athol Fugard and John Kani have received critical acclaim in New York, London and elsewhere.

The performing arts have a strong base and long tradition in South Africa and perhaps reached their peak in the last years of apartheid when theatre gave voice to protest that would otherwise have been silenced.

The Market Theatre complex in Johannesburg and others risked closure by running some political performances. Today that courage has been transformed into a desire to teach, and many theatres run courses helping train aspiring actors.

Every year in June, Grahamstown in the Eastern Cape runs a week-long arts festival *(see Eastern Cape section, pp38–43)* where both established and fringe actors, playwrights and other performers strut their stuff. Various smaller festivals are hosted elsewhere in the country *(see pp24–5)*.

African Footprint, a big, bold African musical, was a huge success and even played in China.

Various symphony orchestras perform regularly, and some of the larger cities host ballets and opera, often with international guest artists performing. In poor areas, many churches and other groups run choirs which give public performances, an easy way of helping to create pride and status for people who struggle to make a daily living.

ART

Perhaps some of the most unusual art galleries in the country are the rock overhangs and shelters where San (Bushmen) artists used vegetable and animal blood paints to record hunting, ceremonies and other scenes.

The San wandered through South Africa as long as 40,000 years ago, and left one of the largest collections of rock art in the world scattered throughout the more mountainous areas of South Africa.

Their paintings and rock engraving tell stories of their daily life, but they also had spiritual significance. The richest collections are found in the uKhahlamba-Drakensberg mountains in the Eastern Cape and KwaZulu-Natal.

Museum Africa, Newtown, Johannesburg

Festivals

Most festivals in South Africa are modern events and few have the ancient traditions of those in Europe, Asia or South America. This does not detract from the fun though, and many festivals, and some sporting events, are a good excuse for a party, something South Africans find hard to resist.

Not all festivals are held annually, and it is a good idea to check with tourism authorities about events planned in each region.

Gumboot dancers strut their stuff at a parade

January
Cape Town New Year Carnival
Thousands of singing, dancing minstrels move through the streets of Cape Town. Everyone parties.

February
Dias Festival
Mossel Bay. Food and cultural festival.

Cape Town New Year Carnival, Cape town

March
Klein Karoo National Arts Festival
Afrikaans cultural festival with theatre, music and other entertainment in Oudtshoorn.
Cape Town Festival
Art, music and other events.

April
Rand Show
A huge consumer show with everything from cars and computers to candyfloss. Held in Johannesburg.
North Sea Jazz festival
Cape Town. Two days of world-class jazz. Billed as 'Africa's Grandest Event'.
Port Elizabeth's Splash Festival
Water sport, music and other events.

May
Sabie Forest Fair
Mpumalanga. Various events.

June
Paternoster Seafood Festival
Western Cape. Lots of fresh seafood, wine and music.

July
National Arts Festival
Grahamstown. The biggest event of its kind in South Africa. Theatre, music and other entertainment.
Knysna Oyster Festival
Knysna. Road-running marathons, bicycle races, oysters and other food. The town is usually packed.

August
Winter Witblits Festival
Prince Albert. *Witblits* is powerful home-brewed alcohol, but the festival is also about food and fun.

September
Hello Darling Arts Festival
Darling, Western Cape.
Hermanus Whale Festival
Hermanus. Coincides with peak whale-viewing times. Lots of events.

October
Stellenbosch Food and Wine Festival
Stellenbosch.
Tulbagh Festival
Tulbagh, Western Cape.
Various events.
Jacaranda Festival
Pretoria. Various events.

November
Cherry Festival
Ficksburg, Free State. To celebrate the cherry harvest.

December
Knysna Street Carnival
Holiday crowds having fun.
Spier Summer Arts Festival
Runs until March. Concerts and other entertainment.

The North Sea Jazz Festival, Cape Town

Wildlife

The bio-diversity of southern Africa is extraordinarily varied. Although it only comprises around one per cent of the Earth's landmass, the region hosts more than 340 mammal species, which is about eight per cent of the worldwide total. South Africa also hosts about 880 bird species, and more than one quarter of all living land tortoise species. Altogether more than 400 species of reptile occur in southern Africa – by comparison around 300 species are found in the whole of mainland United States of America.

South Africa's biological diversity is due to the wide variety of habitats that occur in the region. They range from the *fynbos* (a group of plants of which 67 per cent occur only in South Africa) of the western and southern Cape, to sub-tropical coastal forest in KwaZulu-Natal, grasslands in the central regions and savannah in the north and northwest.

Additionally, two ocean currents flow along South Africa's coastline influencing both marine and terrestrial life. The warm sub-tropical Agulhas Current surges down the east coast, while the cold, nutrient-rich Benguela nourishes sealife and influences weather patterns along the west coast.

Game reserves are sprinkled across

the country, each with its own treasures and attractions. South Africa is one of the easiest places in Africa to see 'The Big Five': elephant; lion; rhino (both black and white); leopard and buffalo.

Although these, and predators including the cheetah and wild dog, are considered to be the glamour species, many antelope and smaller species are no less interesting and deserving of attention. The very common impala, zebra, giraffe, wildebeest, baboons, warthogs and dozens of other species all fill important ecological niches and provide endless photo opportunities.

In case these creatures do not provide adequate entertainment, South Africa has many even less well-known animals. Who would not be delighted to spot a pygmy hairy-footed gerbil, a tiny 25gm (one-ounce) rodent that lives in the western parts of South Africa, or even the short-snouted elephant shrew that lives in the hot, dry northern parts of the country?

Birds also range from the large and spectacular to the tiny and unobtrusive. The large eagles and vultures usually occur in game reserves and remote areas where food is plentiful. Lappet-faced and Cape vultures, both with wingspans of over 2,5m (8ft2,5in), martial, bateleur and black-breasted snake eagles excite even experienced birders. Less dramatic are hundreds of other species including the colourful lesser double-collared sunbird and the unobtrusive fairy flycatcher, which tips the scales at just over 8gm (little more than a third of an ounce).

Also at the diminutive end of the scale is the world smallest tortoise, the speckled padloper, which measures just 10cm (almost 4in) across its carapace. This tortoise, which occurs only in the Western Cape, is threatened both by habitat loss and the pet trade.

Whales and dolphins are plentiful in South African waters, and in season are easily and often seen from the shore. *(see whale-watching feature on pp122–3).*

A large number of excellent guidebooks covering mammals, birds, reptiles, trees and other subjects are available in South African book shops *(see directory on p142).*

Copyright: South African Tourism

Opposite: Female elephants are very protective towards their young
Above: The fastest land mammal, the cheetah, can reach a speed of 100kph (62mph)

Some Common Animals of the Bush

Although spotting the 'Big Five' is the highlight of a visit to the bush, there are many other animals, which are no less interesting and will almost certainly be seen more often.

They all play an important role in the jigsaw puzzle of ecosystems – remove one species entirely and it affects the whole picture.

Cheetah

With its long legs and lithe body the cheetah is clearly built for speed – a design which has made it the fastest mammal on Earth. Cheetahs hunt small antelope, and sometimes prey as small as rabbits, by slowly stalking them and then bursting into an explosive sprint. They tire quickly and not every hunt is successful. Cheetahs are the slightest of the large cats, with males weighing up to 60kg (132lb), and are often robbed of their kills by spotted hyaenas, leopards and, sometimes, lions.

Copyright: South African Tourism

Giraffe

Besides their obvious size and height – males weigh up to1,200kg (2,640lb) and stand 5m (16ft3in) tall – giraffe,

when seen up close, have wonderfully long eyelashes. Nobody is sure why this is so, but it might be to protect their eyes when browsing on thorn trees. They are common in many of the game reserves, particularly in the northern and eastern parts of the country.

Copyright: South African Tourism

Impala

The graceful impala is one of the most common animals in the Kruger National Park and many other game reserves. Many people simply drive past them because they are so common, but it's well worth spending time watching them.

Most lambs are born in November, and a couple of months later can be seen gathered together in nursery groups within the herd. Only males have horns.

Kudu

The tall, handsome kudu is the most common of all the large antelope and sometimes lives quite close to farmhouses and other human habitation. The males have beautiful

to drink water for most of the year, deriving all their moisture requirements from their food. Gemsbok also have very sophisticated body-cooling systems and water utilisation abilities.

long, spiralled horns. Kudu usually live in small herds.

Springbok

South Africa's national animal prefers the drier central and western regions of the country. They used to form herds hundreds of thousands strong as they followed the rains, which generate fresh grazing. Today their population is much smaller, but springbok are common enough in game reserves and on many farms.

Gemsbok

Long, rapier-like horns are the most obvious feature of this large, powerful antelope. It too is a creature of the drier areas and happily survives in the middle of the Kalahari Desert. They do not need

Spotted Hyaena

These powerful predators have had a bad press and are not in any way as cowardly as they are so often portrayed in popular stories and movies. They often hunt for themselves and can bring down prey as large as a wildebeest weighing over 200kg (440lb).

Nevertheless, they are very effective scavengers too, and use their immensely powerful jaws to tear skin and crack bone that not even lions can handle.

Steenbok

These tiny antelope are common in many parts of South Africa. They are often seen in the same area because they form territories which they defend against other steenbok. They only weigh about 11kg (24lb).

Impressions

South Africa is an easy country to visit. All the major centres are linked by regular flights, the road system is good, and there are excellent hotels, B&Bs, game reserves and national parks. All the major centres have a wide range of well-stocked shops, medical care is first class and the telephone system and internet facilities are the best in Africa. The tourism industry has grown by leaps and bounds in recent years and service standards are good.

The Victoria & Alfred Waterfront, Cape Town

Climate

Cape Town and the southern Cape coast have a Mediterranean climate with warm to hot summers and mild to cool winters, which is when most of the rainfall occurs. Elsewhere in South Africa, most rainfall occurs in summer.

In many parts of the interior of the country it can become very hot in summer, particularly in the Kruger National Park, Kgalagadi Transfrontier Park and parts of KwaZulu-Natal.

Johannesburg is the economic and industrial heart of South Africa

Winter days in the interior are cool, but at night the temperature can fall below freezing. The coastal belt of KwaZulu-Natal is very humid in summer.

School Holidays

Most South Africans take their annual holidays over Christmas or Easter, and more popular destinations are accordingly very busy. Although the crowds create an exciting atmosphere, tourists with some flexibility in their schedule might want to avoid these peak periods.

What to Take

All the major cities are well stocked with almost any item of clothing or equipment the average traveller might need – so should anything be forgotten there is no need to panic.

Health

Good medical care and hospitals are available throughout South Africa *(see box on AIDS on p13)*. Consult your doctor or a travel clinic about anti-malaria medication if you intend

Cape Town's Long Street has something for everyone

visiting the hot northern and northeastern parts of the country, particularly the Kruger National Park and the game reserves of northern KwaZulu-Natal. All tap water is drinkable. Use sunscreen, even in winter, as South Africa has very high rates of ultra-violet radiation.

Access for Disabled Persons

Although some buildings and public areas have been made user-friendly to disabled people, this is not widespread. Larger airports have been designed or adapted to assist disabled people.

Getting Around

- All the larger centres are linked by air, and rental cars are easily hired at airports.
- Public transport is not good, and in smaller centres or rural areas taxi services are poor.
- It is best to make transport arrangements at the hotel or B&B and to take advantage of local knowledge.
- Avoid the ubiquitous minibus taxis, unless you are prepared to endure bad driving and poorly maintained vehicles.
- Several reputable companies operate long-distance coaches between major centres, but be aware that distances can be intimidating. Cape Town, for

The Tsitsikamma mountains on the Garden Route

example, is 1,500km (940 miles) from Johannesburg.

• There are tolls on major roads. Cash or credit cards are accepted.

• South Africa has an extensive rail system linking all the major centres. The luxurious Blue Train runs between Cape Town and Johannesburg, and is an easy way of seeing some of the countryside in comfort.

Self Drive

It is a good idea to carry a cellular phone in case of a breakdown or some other emergency. Programme important numbers like that of the car rental company, the Automobile Association and your hotel into the phone so you can find help easily should you experience a breakdown.

South Africans are, as a rule, poor drivers so exercise caution on the roads. Should the driver of the minibus taxi

Copyright: South African Tourism

Transport takes many forms in South Africa

travelling in front of you activate the hazard lights on his vehicle, it means he is about to stop, whether it is legal or not, to collect or drop off passengers. Be alert. (On major routes drivers sometimes use their emergency flashers as a means of thanking you for allowing them to pass.)

Urban myth says that, because of the crime rate, people may feel unsafe and it is therefore acceptable to stop at red traffic lights late at night, and then continue on your way if the road is clear. It is not acceptable, and it is illegal. Wait for the green.

Crime

This subject is always at the top of most people's list of concerns. Yes, South Africa does have an abnormally high crime rate, but the best protection against criminals is common sense. Tens of millions of South Africans use this tactic on a daily basis.

Take sensible precautions as you would anywhere else in the world, and, if in doubt, ask your hotel, B&B or tour guide for advice.

• If you are ever in the unfortunate position of having someone armed with a weapon attempting to steal your car or anything else, never ever resist. The situation is unlikely to arise but, if it does, let the thieves take whatever they want.

• Don't carry unnecessary cash or valuables, and do not leave cameras or bags on the seat of your car. Store them out of sight, preferably in the boot. Lock your doors.

• It is best to take tours to some areas rather than drive yourself. Again, ask advice. Avoid self-appointed 'guides' who approach you in the street.

While it is important to be alert, remember the vast majority of tourists never experience crime so don't let the subject dominate your holiday.

Visiting Game Reserves and Dealing with Wildlife

Never feed wild animals, whether in game reserves or not, because the animals begin to associate humans with food. This later causes conflict with humans, and authorities end up having to shoot problem animals that are a threat. Human food also creates health problems in wild animals.

• Baboons and monkeys are particularly good at begging, extremely clever, strong, very fast and take advantage of humans in a flash. No matter how cute they appear to be, do not feed them.

• Don't get out of the car in Big Five game reserves as some species are potentially dangerous.

• If you encounter elephants while driving in a game reserve, always give them space to move off, and do not get between adults and babies. They are usually accustomed to cars and pose no threat, but it is best to give them space.

• If you have been walking through long grass, check your legs and arms for ticks afterwards. Several anti-tick sprays are available.

• Most mosquitoes start biting in the evening, so it is a good idea to wear long trousers and long sleeves if you want to avoid getting bitten. Use mosquito repellents too.

Baboons have become used to humans and are pests in some areas

Language

South Africa has 11 official languages, and a list of useful phrases in all 11 would take up half this book.

English is widely spoken, and nearly all signage is in English. Other languages, including Afrikaans, Zulu and Xhosa, sometimes appear on signboards.

For the record, the 11 languages are English, Afrikaans, Ndebele, Northern Sotho (Pedi), Siswati, Southern Sotho, Tsonga, Tswana, Venda, Xhosa and Zulu.

Etiquette

South Africans are generally friendly and welcoming towards tourists. Most people are willing to offer advice and suggestions and are happy to chat with foreigners about sport, politics or whatever subject seems appropriate.

The popular seaside town of Hermanus

A friendly "Hi, how are you?" will elicit an acknowledgement and probably the same question in response which forms a good platform for any conversation.

When meeting people, a handshake is a widely accepted form of greeting. Some Black people use a more complicated handshake, which involves the standard grip, and then, without releasing, slipping your hand around the other person's thumb, then returning to the traditional grasp.

Money

Travellers' cheques are accepted in most banks, and credit cards are used throughout the country. Credit cards are not accepted for fuel. Most banks issue a separate card for fuel purchases.

Clothing

The South African lifestyle is fairly casual. In summer, many people wear shorts, casual shirts, and sandals, particularly at the coast and in game reserves. For those unused to harsh sunlight, it is wise to remember to use sunscreen on legs and arms when wearing shorts and T-shirts. Dress in good restaurants is slightly more formal, but jackets and ties are unnecessary unless on business.

Before you Leave

Visit the South African Tourism website to catch up on links to the latest shows, big sporting matches and other events that will add to the enjoyment of your trip.

South Africa Tourism
Tel: (011) 895 3000.
www.SouthAfrica.net

Quiet and peaceful Swellendam is one of the oldest towns in South Africa

Visitors to South Africa are often confused by the reference to 'townships' rather than suburbs or cities. Although Soweto is a huge area with a population of millions, it is usually referred to as a 'township in Johannesburg' but is in reality part of the same conurbation. The same rule applies to Kwa-Mashu near Durban, Zwide near Port Elizabeth and Mamelodi near Pretoria.

As with many things in South Africa, townships came about as a result of the apartheid policy of separate development – segregating people on the grounds of race – and were created as residential areas exclusively for Black people. Black people were only allowed into the formerly 'White' cities to provide labour, and apartheid planners decided that housing and other facilities were to be kept at the most basic level

possible. Most houses were tiny, almost square 'matchbox' houses with no electricity and no running water inside the houses. Toilets were built outside and used a night soil system where tankers collected buckets of sewage a few times a week. Initially, most roads were unpaved and street lighting was non-existent.

In terms of the policies of 'separate development', Black people needed a permit to be in White urban areas, and White people needed special permission from the authorities to visit townships. Neither permit was easy to obtain and applications were often denied. Even today many White South Africans have never visited a township despite working or playing sport with people who have lived there all their lives. Most townships were originally built with few access roads to make it easy for police to monitor comings and goings. Because the townships were intended as labour dormitories, almost no formal commercial developments such as supermarkets were allowed, forcing Black people to shop 'in town' – usually the nearest city.

Today townships are changing daily with increasing numbers of urban people having access to electricity, telephones and running water, and most roads are now tarred. Some of the informal settlements that have sprung up in and near townships still lack even these basics.

It may seem odd to treat townships as tourist attractions because, quite obviously, they are not galleries or museums. The experience is, however, well worth the time because Gugulethu is a vastly different place to the suburbs of Cape Town, as are the streets of Mamelodi and Pretoria. Every city has several townships, usually hidden out of the way, and even small towns have their own 'townships'.

They are usually lively, friendly places where everyone seems to know everyone else, a characteristic often lacking in the some of the formerly 'Whites-only' suburbs in many South African cities. Kids yell as they play soccer in the streets, and enterprising mechanics and welders repair cars at the street side while customers wait. Noisy *shebeens* (formerly illegal bars but still called *shebeens* even though they are now legal) are scattered along busy roads. People socialise easily and, on Sunday, many people dressed in their best outfits chat in the streets while walking to church. A tour to a township is an essential, entertaining and educational trip and should not be missed.

www.gauteng.net

Opposite: Fruit seller in Soweto
Above: Soweto is the largest township in South Africa and is home to millions of people

Eastern Cape

Eastern Cape locals are often quietly smug that 'their' broad beaches, numerous mountain ranges and historical sites are seldom deluged with the crowds that Cape Town or Durban sometimes receive. The residents and tourism authorities here are only too happy to welcome tourists, but they are quick to point out that their province is a good place to 'get away from it all'. The climate is mild and ideal for holidays all year round.

www.ecapetourism.co.za

Port Elizabeth

Although a fairly sedate provincial city, Port Elizabeth is well placed to make the most of good but quiet beaches and interesting history-rich countryside. The city also makes a good base from which to visit the Addo Elephant National Park and the scenic Baviaanskloof Wilderness Area.

The area saw the first meetings, and clashes, between Khoikhoi, British, Dutch, German and Xhosa people. The 1820 settlers from Britain landed here, and there are still many well-preserved buildings from the era throughout the region.

Tourism Port Elizabeth
Tel: (041) 585 8884.
www.ibhayi.com

The Nelson Mandela Metropolitan Art Museum (formerly King George VI Art Museum and Gallery)

The museum houses various exhibitions from the Eastern Cape and elsewhere in South Africa, as well as international art, including Chinese textiles and Indian miniature figurines.

1 Park Dr, Port Elizabeth 6001. Tel: (041) 586 1030. www.artmuseum.co.za Open: Mon–Fri 8.30am–5pm, Sat & Sun 2pm–5pm. First Sun of the month 9am–5pm, when art exhibitions are held in the park outside the museum.

Grahamstown's Cathedral dominates the skyline

No 7 Castle Hill Museum

This museum is housed in one of the oldest settler cottages in Port Elizabeth. The cottage was built in 1827 and has been restored to its original state. Various displays reflect the lifestyle of the 1820 settlers.

7 Castle Hill, Central.
Tel: (041) 582 2515.
Open: Mon–Fri 10am–4.30pm.

Bayworld Complex

Dolphins, fossils and reptiles are all features of this complex, which unsurprisingly incorporates a museum, dolphinarium and snake park.

The museum exhibits a wide range of natural and cultural history displays, and the dolphinarium presents daily shows. Nearby the snake park has an impressive range of residents.

Humewood. Tel: (041) 584 0650.
Open: Mon–Sun 9am–4.40pm.
Call to confirm times of dolphin shows.

Grahamstown

Today Grahamstown is a small university town, but in the early 18th century it was a turbulent frontier post where European settlers clashed regularly with the Xhosa over land and cattle.

The Cathedral is the focal point of the town which has many old buildings that have been restored to their original condition. Several museums explain both social and natural history. The South African Institute for Aquatic Diversity is the most unusual, and contains one of the most comprehensive exhibits of aquatic life ever collected.

During university term, students throng the streets of the town and give pubs and restaurants a lively, cheerful atmosphere. Between 27 June and 6 July the town hosts South Africa's largest arts and theatre festival, which attracts thousands of visitors.

Grahamstown Tourism

63 High St. Tel: (046) 622 3241.
info@grahamstown.com

National Arts Festival

Tel: (046) 622 7115. Held in July. Call to confirm dates and bookings.

1820s Settlers' National Monument and Memorial Museum

Houses a collection of artefacts from the time, ranging from toys to weapons.

South African Institute for Aquatic Diversity

Somerset Ave.
Tel: (046) 636 1002.
www.jlbsmith.ru.ac.za
Open: Mon–Fri 8am–5pm.

Informal traders in East London

Traders on East London Beach

Addo Elephant National Park

Originally created in 1931 to protect the last 11 elephants found in the region, this reserve has recently been expanded and has a healthy population of more than 340 animals.

This is the largest elephant population south of those in the Kruger National Park and KwaZulu-Natal. The thick vegetation also supports black rhino, antelope and other smaller creatures. *Addo is about 70km northwest of Port Elizabeth.*

National Parks Board Central Reservations
Tel: (012) 428 9111.
www.parks-sa.co.za
Open all year.

East London, Port Alfred and King William's Town

Wide, open beaches and pleasant farming land make this region popular as a family holiday destination. There are many good swimming beaches, hiking trails and nature reserves.

King William's Town is a former frontier outpost where the Xhosa and Khoikhoi people often clashed with settlers. The excellent Amathole Museum has a collection of exhibits of 19th Century life and Xhosa culture, as well as a large collection of South African mammals. Huberta, a hippo that walked more than 1,000km (629 miles) down the South African coast in the late 1920s and early 1930s, is preserved here. (Nobody knows why she decided to walk that far.) The East London Museum contains the world's only dodo egg and also has a preserved specimen of a coelacanth *(see box on p43).*

East London City hall

East London Museum
Entrance in Dawson St.
Tel: (043) 743 0686.
Open: Mon–Fri 9.30am–5pm, Sat
2pm–5pm, Sun & public holidays
11am–4pm.
Closed: Christmas Day & Good Friday.
Small admission charge.

Anne Bryant Art Gallery
Upper Oxford St.
Tel: (0431) 722 4044.
Open: Mon–Fri 9am–5pm Sat & public
holidays 9am–12pm. Closed: Christmas
Day & New Year's Day.
Admission charge.

Calgary Transport Museum
13km from East London on N6 to
Stutterheim.

Tel: (043) 730 7244.
Open: daily 9am–4pm.
Closed: Good Friday & Christmas Day.
Small admission charge.

Amathole Museum
Albert St, King William's Town.
Tel: (043) 642 4506.
Open: Mon–Sat 9am–4.30pm, Sun
10am–3pm.

Gately House
1 Park Gates Rd. Tel: (043) 722 2141.
Open: Tues–Thurs 10am–1pm &
2pm–5pm, Fri 10am–1pm, Sat & Sun
3pm–5pm.
Admission by donation.

Wild Coast
This remote coastline of sea cliffs, broad

Graaff Reinet's Cathedral is a copy of Salisbury Cathedral in England

lagoons and open countryside runs from just north of East London all the way to KwaZulu-Natal.

A variety of hotels and smaller lodges are dotted all the way along the coast. The coast is still relatively undeveloped and suits more adventurous tourists looking for a quiet beach holiday away from the main tourism beat.

Although this area is a good holiday destination, it is also the graveyard of many ships, wrecked by the powerful currents and heavy seas that sometimes occur along this coast.

Wild Coast Tourism
Tel: (047) 531 5290.
www.ectourism.co.za

Amatola Mountains and Hogsback

These mountains, some 200km (125 miles) north of Port Elizabeth and 120km (75 miles) northwest of East London, are one of South Africa's better-kept secrets. Many parts of the range are grasslands, and there are extensive forests which are ideal for hiking, climbing, mountain biking and fly-fishing.

A B&B in the lush Hogsback region

The region is rich in Xhosa culture, and the nearby University of Fort Hare houses an important collection of African art. The village of Hogsback is quaintly reminiscent of England, and makes a good base to explore the region. There are no fewer than 23 waterfalls in the area.

Hogsback Tourism Bureau
Tel: (045) 962 1340.

Mountain Zebra National Park

This park was originally established to save the Cape mountain zebra from extinction. It has succeeded in that goal to the point that some animals have been relocated to repopulate other Karoo parks.

Nature trails and walks cross the 6,536-hectare reserve, and a good variety of wildlife including kudu, springbok and birds occur.

Booking through SA National Parks Central Reservations
Tel: (012) 428 9111.
Open: all year round.

Graaff Reinet

Many of Graaff Reinet's historic flat-roofed Karoo cottages, Cape Dutch and Victorian buildings have been colourfully restored. The town makes an eye-catching contrast to the semi-desert scrub that covers the mountains around the town.

The Grootkerk (large church) is a copy of the Salisbury Cathedral in England, and the Drostdy Hotel has been restored to its 1806 grandeur. More than 200 buildings in the town have been declared national monuments. The Old Library houses a large collection of fossils, and Reinet House, which is

The Owl House, Nieu-Bethesda

claimed to have the world's largest living grape vine in the garden, is a museum with displays explaining the region's history. The town was founded in 1786.

Graaff Reinet Publicity Association
Tel: (049) 892 4248.

JH Pierneef Museum
Tel: (049) 892 6107.
Open: Mon–Fri 8am–5pm, Sat & Sun 9am–12pm.

Reinet House
Tel: (049) 892 3801.
Opening times as above.
www.graaffreinet.com

Close to Graaff Reinet

55km north of Graaff Reinet (this is close in Karoo terms) is the small village of Nieu-Bethesda where the Owl House is a monument to the reclusive sculptor Helen Martins (1898–1976). Hundreds of her sculptures of owls, animals and people fill the garden, while the inside of the house is a dream world of murals, mirrors and eerie lighting.

Other artists have since moved to the remote town to enjoy the peace and inspiration of the Sneeuberg mountains and wide-open spaces of the Karoo.

Ibis Art Centre
Nieu-Bethesda.
Tel: (049) 641 1623. (The centre doubles as the tourism bureau.)

The Karoo Nature Reserve
Some 16km (10 miles) outside Graaff Reinet, the Valley of Desolation offers fantastic views across the plains and mountain ranges of the Karoo. The region is rich in fossils, a legacy of the period more than 300 million years ago when marshes and moist forests covered the landscape.

Graaff Reinet Publicity Association
Tel: (049) 892 4248.

Coelacanth display, East London Museum

THE COELACANTH

In 1938 the modern world's first coelacanth *(Latimeria chalumnae)* was caught off the East London coast. Previously it had only been known from fossil remains, although in recent years scientists and fishermen have caught more specimens. It is a fish with fins that resemble primitive stump-like legs – hence ichthyologists affectionately referring to the fish as 'old four legs'.

Free State

The Free State is a quiet agricultural province where everything moves along at a sedate rural pace. Even the citizens of the capital city Bloemfontein don't pay too much attention to the world rushing by – they're too happy enjoying the nearby wide open spaces and blue skies. Most tourists head for the mountainous south-east, but there are rewarding cultural sites, museums and other attractions all over the province.

Clarens

The wide-open grasslands and maize fields of the central Free State give way to mountains and sandstone bluffs near the pretty village of Clarens close to the Lesotho border.

The town has become an artists' haven, and dozens of galleries have sprung up in the town, which is rapidly becoming a favourite weekend haunt. The Easter weekend is the busiest of the year.

The clear, cold streams and mountain air make for good biking, horse riding, hiking and trout fishing.

Clarens Publicity Association
Tel: (058) 256 1542.

A mural in Clarens, Free State

Golden Gate National Park

Set in amongst sandstone mountains with crystal-clear streams and dams, the park offers excellent walking, hiking and horse riding. San hunters used to shelter here, and a variety of grassland game species still occur. Winters can be cold with snowfalls.

The Park is very close to Clarens and it is worth visiting both areas during the same trip. The nearby Qwaqwa Mountain Park is undeveloped but offers good mountain scenery. There is a Basotho cultural village, which depicts traditional life.

The small town of Clarens in the Free State has become a popular weekend destination

South African National Parks' Central Reservations
Tel: (012) 428 9111.
Nearby are the QwaQwa National Park and the Sterkfontein Dam Nature Reserve.

Bloemfontein

In Afrikaaans the name Bloemfontein means 'flower spring', and in Sotho the area was known as Manguang, 'the place of leopards'. Today the settlement has grown into the largest city in the Free State.

There are several museums and monuments, but the most significant is the National Women's Monument and War Museum which commemorates the approximately 26,000 Boer women and children who died in British concentration camps during the South African War of 1899–1902. An estimated 14,000 Black people accused of being Boer sympathisers died in separate camps.
Bloemfontein Publicity Association
Tel: (051) 405 8489.
www.bloemfontein.co.za

National Museum
Corner Charles St and Aliwal St.
Tel: (051) 447 9609. Mon–Fri 8am–5pm, Sat 10am–5pm, Sun 12am–5pm.

Freshford House
31 Kellner St. Tel: (051) 447 9609.
Mon–Fri 10am–1pm, Sat 2pm–5pm.

National Women's War Memorial and War Museum
Monument Rd. Tel: (051) 447 3447.
Open: Mon–Fri. 10am–5pm, Sat 8am–4.30pm, Sun 2pm–5pm.

Sandstone bluffs dominate the scenery of the eastern Free State

THE GREAT TREK

In 1835, two groups of Dutch-speaking Boers left the Cape for the unknown interior in the Great Trek. They felt that the colonial government had failed to provide protection against the Xhosa in the never-ending battle for land, while the abolition of slavery had robbed them of valued possessions.

One group of Voortrekkers, led by Piet Retief, went into Zululand where Dingane massacred their advance party. Revenge was the horrible Battle of Blood River, followed by the establishment of the Republic of Natalia (1838), which Britain annexed. The Boers then trekked north and, in 1860, founded the South African Republic (ZAR). The other party of Voortrekkers trekked beyond the Vaal and Orange rivers and proclaimed the Orange Free State (1854).

Copyright: South African Tourism

Tel: (012) 315 8242.
Bookable in the UK through Thomas
Cook Holidays. Tel: 01733 418650.
www.rovos.co.za

Shongololo Express

Named after a local millipede, this
service offers luxurious train rides taking
in all the highlights of South Africa from
the Kruger National Park to Cape Town.
The trains also travel to Nambia.

KZN Natal Train Tours

Tel: (031) 266 7716.
www.kzntraintours.co.za

S outh Africa is one of the few
remaining countries where you can
still experience magical railway journeys
in trains of enormous prestige. Make an
epic journey conjuring up the romance
of a lost age of steam travel, or take a
short trip for just a day out or a
weekend away.

Under Steam

The Epic Journey
Rovos Rail

The magnificently restored, privately
owned Pride of Africa, travels a variety of
routes. From Cape Town, destinations
include Victoria Falls (Zimbabwe) and Dar
es Salaam (Tanzania), with stopovers at
Matjiesfontein, Kimberley and Pretoria,
and optional sightseeing en route.

Sleepers, dining car and observation
carriages are the refurbished originals, a
reminder of pre-war opulence.

Union Limited

A steam locomotive and original
carriages of the old Union Limited, the
first luxury train (1923) taking first-class
passengers from Johannesburg to Cape
Town to meet the ocean liners, have
been transformed into a 'safari' train
with a variety of routes and destinations.

Transnet

Tel: (011) 773 9523.
www.transnetheritagefoundation.co.za

Short Excursions

Banana Express

The Banana Express steams its way
through coastal hills and sugar-cane
fields to the Oribi Gorge Nature Reserve.
The round trip takes a few hours and
makes a good day out.
Tel: (039) 682 4821. Call to confirm
schedule.

Magaliesberg Express

The South African National Railway and Steam Museum Preservation Group offers day trips from Johannesburg Station to the Magaliesberg (see p60).

Magaliesberg Tourism
Tel: (012) 888 1154.
www.magaliesberg.co.za. Call to confirm schedule.

Die Herrie

Operating between Oudtshoorn and Calitzdorp, the train traverses ostrich country and the Karoo.
Tel: (044) 272 2377. Call to confirm schedule.

Outeniqua Choo-Tjoe

This distinguished old steam train covers the George to Knysna section of the Garden Route (see Garden Route feature on pp134–7), and is probably one of the country's most enjoyable services, passing through spectacular scenery.
Tel: (044) 801 8228.
Mon–Sat, but call to confirm schedule. 4–6 hour round trip.

The Apple Express

The Apple Express runs from Port Elizabeth, and crosses the historic Van Staden's river bridge, the highest narrow-gauge railway bridge in the world.
Tel: (041) 583 2620.
www.appleexpress.com

Diesel or Electric Train Travel

The Blue Train

The Blue Train replaced the old Johannesburg-Cape Town Union Limited train in 1939. Its name derives from the colour of the old original train. Today's Blue Train is one of the great trains of the world, a slower alternative to flying (Cape Town-Pretoria, 24 hours), but an infinitely superior experience. It has sleeping accommodation with showers, a dining and lounge car, and space to carry cars. An additional new Transvaal Lowveld Route, Pretoria to Nelspruit, is an excellent springboard for visits to the Kruger National Park. There are also trips to Victoria Falls in Zimbabwe.
Tel: (021) 334 8459.
www.bluetrain.com
Bookable in the UK through Thomas Cook Holidays. Tel: 01733 418650.

Regular Passenger Services

Regular inter-city trains traverse some amazing landscapes. The best routes are the Trans-Karoo, the Trans-Orange, the Trans-KZN and the Algoa Express. There are a variety of discounts for children and senior citizens.

Transnet
Tel: Toll free 086 000 8888.
If calling from outside South Africa.
Tel: (012) 315 2757.

Opposite: Steam Train, Knysna, Western Cape

Gauteng

Almost 120 years ago, the world's richest gold deposits were discovered near what is today Johannesburg. Prospectors, speculators and the merely hopeful flocked from across the globe to the sweeping grasslands and ridges of the South African Highveld in search of quick success and, sadly for most, elusive fortunes. Today, the concrete, steel and glass office towers and efficient infrastructure of Johannesburg, its glitzy sister city Sandton and nearby Pretoria act as similar symbols of hope, offering jobs and opportunity to people from all over southern Africa.

Gauteng is the economic heartland of South Africa and, although it is the country's smallest province, it generates more than a third of the nation's gross domestic product (GDP).

Office blocks dominate the skyline of wealthy Sandton

The region is home to some of the most powerful mining companies in the world, and boasts the largest concentration of technology, financial services and manufacturing expertise in Africa.

Gauteng has a long history of human habitation, and archaeologists have unearthed some of the world's oldest hominid fossils dating back some 3,3 million years at several sites – most notably at the Sterkfontein Caves, 45 minutes north of central Johannesburg.

The climate is comfortable, with warm summers and cool, clear winters, although the region's high altitude – it is on average about 1,600m (5,200ft) above sea level – sometimes results in icy nights.

JOHANNESBURG AND SANDTON

Johannesburg and its satellite city Sandton are the symbols of the upwardly mobile in South Africa.

Nelson Mandela Square in Sandton

A widespread perception is that everything happens faster, and that everything is bigger and better than elsewhere. This belief is reflected in the expensive cars, big houses, fashionable shops and upmarket restaurants. But the region is also one of many contrasts. Just as the stores in Sandton carry famous clothing labels and jewellery brands, shops in the nearby dormitory areas of Soweto and Alexandra stock only basic foods and other household essentials.

A tour to Soweto or Alexandra provides an important insight into the development of South Africa, and also offers a glimpse of energetic, largely cheerful township life.

Downtown Johannesburg bustles with traders and shoppers from throughout the region. Colourful fabrics decorate storefronts, and informal chefs roast *mealies* (corn) on street corners. Hundreds of minibus taxis piled high with goods leave crowded ranks to ferry people around the metropolis, to rural areas and to countries as far away as Zimbabwe and Zambia.

An evening spent at the Market Theatre or a club in the Newtown Precinct will confirm the cultural diversity of the city, as will a visit to the sidewalk cafés in Melville. The fashion conscious-hang out in Nelson Mandela Square or Rivonia Road, or visit the antique shops and cafés of Parkhurst on weekend afternoons.

Surprisingly for such a large, densely populated city, there are many nature reserves. At the Walter Sisulu Botanical Gardens (formerly the Witwatersrand

National Botanical Gardens), carefully tended displays of plants from all over South Africa thrive, while on the cliffs above the rolling lawns a pair of wild black eagles continue to breed, as they have done for more than a decade.

Apartheid Museum

A plethora of multimedia displays take the visitor through the stark cruelty of racial separation enforced by apartheid, but also showcase South Africa's remarkable transition to democracy. The story of political and social upheavals is skilfully told, and provides an invaluable insight into the development of modern South Africa.

Gold Reef Road, Crown Mines
Tel: (011) 309 4700.
www.apartheidmuseum.org

Apartheid Museum, Johannesburg

Open: 10am–5pm. Closed: Mon, Good Friday & Christmas Day.
Admission charge.

Constitution Hill

South Africa's new Constitutional Court has been built here around the notorious former prison called The Fort. Many famous prisoners, including Nelson Mandela and Mahatma Gandhi, were once held in the prison. Various parts of the prison are used as galleries explaining the history of The Fort.
Constitution Hill, Braamfontein.
Gauteng Tourism
Tel: (011) 327 2000.

Gold Reef City

The theme park has been built around an authentic 19th century gold mine. Visitors can travel 200m (650ft) underground down a mine to learn about the industry and the history of South Africa's biggest gold rush. Buildings representative of the period have been restored around the Number 14 Shaft of the original Crown Mines. Various other forms of entertainment are offered, including 'gumboot dancing' made famous by migrant workers on the mines. There is a variety of amusement park rides and a hotel and casino nearby.
Crown Mines. Tel: (011) 248 6800.
www.goldreefcity.co.za
Open: Tues–Sun 9.30am–5pm.
Closed: Mon.

Johannesburg Art Gallery

This large gallery has one of the country's best art collections. Works include those by local and international

artists, both contemporary and classical. Gerard Sekoto, Sydney Kumalo and Alexis Preller are well represented, and there are works by Claude Monet, Edgar Degas and other artists. There are many collections of local beadwork, carving and other exhibits.
Joubert Park. Tel: (011) 725 3130.
It is best to visit with a tour guide as the Joubert Park area is unsafe for tourists.

Markets

Over 500 at the **Rosebank Mall Rooftop Market** stalls offer crafts, arts, books, clothing and food. The market is particularly good for African carvings, masks, figurines and jewellery. Food is available too.
Open: Sun 9am–4pm.

The **African Craft Market** is on the ground floor of the same building and offers similar wares.
Both at Cradock Avenue, Rosebank.
Tel: (011) 442 4488.
www.crafts.co.za
Open: daily 9am–5pm.

The **Bruma Fleamarket** offers a wide variety of goods, including African artwork, carvings and other curios. As with the markets listed above, bargaining is acceptable and expected. There are food stalls, and on weekends and holidays there is entertainment too, often in the form of traditional dancers.
Corner Marcia St and Ernest Oppeneheimer St, Bruma.
Tel: (011) 786 0776.
Open: daily 9am–4pm.

The **Mai Mai Market** specialises in traditional medicines used for both

Zulu trader in the Mai Mai Market, Johannesburg

African Craft Market in Rosebank

physical and spiritual health. The majority of Black people in South Africa consult both Western-style and traditional doctors, and many of the traditional products are available here. Most stallholders will happily explain the myriad uses of plants and animal parts.

The stalls are not for the squeamish, because of the many animal bones, skins and horns on display, but they are an integral part of African culture.

Albert St, near intersection with Berea St, Johannesburg.
Open: Mon–Sat all day. Closed: Sun.
Hard to find, and in a run-down area, so taking a guide is advisable.

Museum Africa

This is Johannesburg's major cultural history museum and is housed in the old Market Building which was built in 1913. Permanent exhibitions include displays of South African rock art, geology, and photography dating back 100 years.

The dangers of mining and the rise of township jazz are among several themes highlighted. The 'Tried for Treason' display tells the story of Nelson Mandela and 155 other prisoners who went on trial in 1956 for their anti-apartheid activities.

121 Bree St, Newtown.
Tel: (011) 833 5624.
Open: 9am–4pm. Closed: Mon, Good Friday, Christmas Day & Day of Goodwill.
Small admission charge.

Sandton

Sandton City, Nelson Mandela Square (formerly Sandton Square) and the nearby Hyde Park Corner Shopping

Centre form the heart of the wealthy shopping areas of the lush northern suburbs. African fashion and influences rub shoulders with imports directly from Europe. The season's trends and famous labels are all important to well-heeled shoppers browsing the boutiques.

Upmarket coffee shops and cafés provide useful vantage points to watch who is buying what, and good bookstores and cinemas offer somewhat more cerebral relaxation.

Sandton City
5th St, Sandton.
Tel: (011) 883 2011.
Open: daily from 8am.

Nelson Mandela Square
5th St, Sandton.
Tel: (011) 784 2750.
Open: daily from 8am.

Hyde Park Corner Shopping Centre
Jan Smuts Ave. Tel: (011) 325 4340.
Open: daily from 8am.

South African Lipizzaners

These powerful white 'dancing horses' are famed for their skill in executing complex movements in the classical traditions invented by Spanish riding masters during the Middle Ages. The Kyalami Centre is the only riding school outside of the Spanish Riding School in Vienna, Austria, with official approval to conduct Lipizzaner performances.

There are 65 of these rare horses based at Kyalami, and every Sunday expert riders put the stallions through their complex routines.
1 Dahlia Rd, Kyalami.
Tel: (011) 702 2103. Shows: Sun 10.30am.
Admission charge.

Shopping at Sandton City, Sandton

THE SOUTH AFRICAN WAR

Following success in the First Anglo-Boer War (1880), the Transvaal Republic regained independence from Britain. By then its gold was attracting droves of foreign prospectors. British imperialists instigated the Jameson Raid (1895), hoping to ignite an uprising followed by the installation of a British administration. Its failure and ensuing events led to the South African War (1899).

President Kruger's commandos defeated the British at Talana Hill and routed them at Nicholson's Nek, but their siege of Ladysmith proved to be disastrous and ultimately cost them the war. By 1900, Pretoria had surrendered. A rural guerrilla war resulted in savage retribution: Boer women and children were imprisoned in the world's first concentration camps. The horror of these led ultimately to the Peace of Vereeniging (1902).

South African National Museum of Military History

This museum contains a unique collection of weaponry and uniforms spanning 120 years of South African military history, including the Anglo-Zulu War, the South African War, the First and Second World Wars and the liberation wars fought during the birth of modern South Africa.

The displays include artillery pieces, tanks and other armoured vehicles, a German-made, two-man mini-submarine and the only preserved World War 2 Messerschmit Me 260 B jet night fighter.

Herman Ekstein Park, (close to the Johannesburg Zoo), entrance intersection Erlswold and Eastwold Avenue, Saxonwold. Tel: (011) 646 1153. Open: daily 9.30am–4.30pm. Admission charge.

Soweto

The vibrant dusty streets of Soweto provide a fascinating insight into the complex world of South African society. Built by apartheid's planners merely to provide labour for industry, Soweto and other townships have a life and culture of their own, and are a world apart from the Western orientation of Johannesburg's more affluent areas.

Much of the struggle against apartheid took place in areas like Soweto, and there are several memorials to those who died, including the Hector Peterson Memorial in Orlando West.

Most tours take in these memorials as well as the former homes of two Nobel Peace Prize winners, Nelson Mandela and Archbishop Desmond Tutu. Both homes are in Vilakazi Street, the only street in the world that can boast two Nobel Prize winners.

Elsewhere, visitors get a flavour of

The sprawling township of Soweto

township life visiting small restaurants or *shebeens* (bars).

Taking an organised tour is advised, and several operators run tours to Soweto, Alexandra and other townships.

Gauteng Tourism
Rosebank Mall.
Tel: (011) 327 2000.
www.gauteng.net

Walter Sisulu National Botanical Gardens

Formerly the Witwatersrand National Botanical Gardens, this 300-hectare (741-acre) area features a variety of walks through the landscaped and natural *veld* areas, which showcase many species of indigenous plants. Over 230 species of birds have been recorded as well as a number of small mammals. The 70m (227ft) high Witpoortjie Falls is visible from most parts of the gardens, which also include a small dam and bird hide.

Walter Sisulu National Botanical Gardens, near Johannesburg

REGINA MUNDI CHURCH

Regina Mundi, sometimes known as 'The Queen of Soweto' is a church that has played a pivotal role in the township's turbulent political history.

During the apartheid years, the huge Catholic Church, which can seat 2,000 people, was often used as a venue for political gatherings, many of which were disrupted by police using tear gas and, in some instances, guns. During the 1976 Soweto uprisings, children wounded by police gunfire took refuge in the church, as did many others in later years.

Today the church, built in 1964, has had a park created in its gardens, and inside the church there is an art gallery featuring the history of Soweto and Johannesburg.

Open-air concerts are held in winter, when the sun is still warm but rain is unlikely, and many bring picnics and sit on the rolling lawns while listening to the music.

Malcom Road, Poortview, Roodepoort.
Tel: (011) 958 1750 or 958 0529.
www.nbi.ac.za
Open: 8am–5pm all year.
Admission charge.

PRETORIA

Pretoria is South Africa's capital but, despite its political importance, this small city moves at a relatively leisurely pace. The city has been the seat of various South African governments for most of the last 110 years beginning with the Boer Republics, which declared independence from Britain in the late 1800s, and most recently the African National Congress-controlled government.

As the home of the country's civil service and international diplomatic corps, it is a fairly staid city, although vibrant pockets of restaurants and clubs keep students and more adventurous officials up until the early hours. The University of Pretoria is one of South Africa's largest, and is known for its wildlife and, in particular, mammal research, and the nearby Transvaal Museum has important collections of a wide range of species.

Various museums and art galleries reflect much of South Africa's past, but also illustrate the constantly developing nature of the country's social and political structure. At the start of the hot summers, much of the city becomes covered in the purple blossom of the jacaranda trees that line many of the wide streets.

Melrose House

Set in verdant gardens, this museum was originally a Victorian home built in 1886. Later it became the headquarters of the British forces fighting against the boers in the South African War of 1899–1902.

Throughout the latter years of the war, generals briefed Queen Victoria from the house, and in 1902 the Treaty of Vereeniging was signed here, ending the conflict.

The architecture of the house and displays of furniture and other *bric-a-brac* provide a good example of the tastes of wealthy Victorian colonial settlers. Displays of period photographs reveal the harsh conditions of this war.

Snacks are served in the gardens. *275 Jacob Maré Street, Pretoria. Tel: (012) 322 0240.*

Union Buildings

Open: Tues–Sun 10am–5pm.
Admission charge.

Pretoria Art Museum

This important museum has fine examples of many forms of South African art, including contemporary work as well as those of older, more established artists.

South Africa's best-known 'old school' painters such as Anton van Wouw, Maggie Loubser, Henk Pierneef and Irma Stern are exhibited, and many prints and other media from the 18th and 19th centuries are also displayed. The gallery highlights the transition of modern South African art away from a purely eurocentric base, and also emphasises the use of more unorthodox media.

218 Vermeulen Street.
Tel: (012) 344 1807.
Open: Tues–Sat 10am–5pm, Sun 12am–5pm. Closed: Mon & public holidays.
Small admission charge.
www.pretoriaartmuseum.co.za

The Union Buildings

Designed by the famous British colonial architect Sir Herbert Baker, and completed in 1913, the Union Buildings have loomed large in the minds of South Africans ever since.

For a long time the seat of the apartheid government, these sandstone buildings represented to many the oppression of apartheid rule. In 1994, it was here that Nelson Mandela was sworn in as president.

Perched on a hill, the buildings and surrounding gardens provide good views of the city.

Tours of the gardens can be arranged Mon–Fri. Contact local tour operators (see directory on p188).

Transvaal Museum

This museum has one of the best collections of southern African birds, mammals, insects and reptiles in the country.

The displays provide a complete overview of nearly all the species most people are likely to see. A wide range of lectures and presentations are offered throughout the year, and special programmes for children are also presented.

It is a working museum, and research staff contribute significantly to the knowledge pool of many species on a regular basis.

Transvaal Museum

Paul Kruger Street, Pretoria.
Tel: (012) 322 7632.
www.nfi.co.za
Open: Mon–Sat 9am–5pm, Sun
11am–5pm. Closed Christmas Day &
Good Friday.

Voortrekker Monument
Just outside Pretoria the huge granite
Voortrekker Monument is visible for
kilometres, and commemorates the
spirit of the Voortrekkers who left the
Cape in 1834. The monument also
depicts a belief that God supported
them in their various battles.
Open: daily 9am–4.30pm.
Admission charge.

FURTHER AFIELD IN GAUTENG

Chameleon Market and Informal
Market
A huge range of African arts and crafts
are available from both the formal and
informal markets here. Weekends are
busy as there are many tourists and
locals on their way to Sun City, or just
enjoying a day in the sun shopping for
bargains. Traders come from as far afield
as Kenya, Senegal and the Democratic
Republic of the Congo, and some of the
goods on sale reflect their origins.
The market is at the foot of Commando
Nek, near the Hartebeespoort Dam wall.
It is 25 minutes from Pretoria and about
50 minutes from Johannesburg. It is a
good place to stop while on the way to Sun
City or the Pilanesberg National Park.

Cradle of Humankind
The area of rocky grass- and shrub-
covered hills and valleys some 45

minutes north of central Johannesburg
has proven to be one of the most
important hominid fossil sites in
the world.
Already more than 500 hominid fossils
and 9,000 stone tools have been
uncovered, including an almost complete
2,6 million-year-old Australopithecine
skull fondly known as 'Mrs Ples'.
There are 12 distinct sites scattered
along the Sterkfontein Valley, including
the Sterkfontein Cave, Wonder Caves
and Swartkrans where there is evidence
of the earliest known deliberate use of
fire about 1,3 million years ago.
Various operators run tours to The
Cradle and there is an excellent
restaurant nearby.
See directory on p188 for tour operators or
contact management for directions. The
Cradle is some 45 minutes north of
central Johannesburg and 35 minutes
north of Sandton.
Tel: (011) 355–1900.
www.cradleofhumankind.co.za
Admission charge.

Crocodile Ramble
This area borders on the Magaliesberg
region, and there are dozens of art
galleries, craft shops, cafés and hotels.

African fabrics

Market near Hartebeespoort Dam

Many people from both Johannesburg and Pretoria spend a Saturday or Sunday wandering around various parts of the ramble area shopping or having tea or lunch. Contact the Ramble tourism office for an electronic or print brochure. Events and exhibitions change regularly. The area also borders on the Cradle of Humankind *(see p58)*.
Tel: (011) 957 3742.
www.crocodileramble.co.za

Cullinan

The largest diamond ever found, the whopping 3,106-carat Cullinan diamond, was found here in 1905. Still a rich source of diamonds, the mine offers regular tours where the mining process – from digging the first hole to cutting the final gem – is explained.

The village has many well-preserved homes and buildings and various museums stores and quiet restaurants help complete a morning or afternoon visit. The village is about

CASINOS

Although a relatively new phenomenon in South Africa (because they were outlawed prior to 1994), casinos are hugely popular, and the spinning wheels and bright lights attract thousands of hopeful customers daily.

The casinos, and accompanying hotels, tend to be situated near the larger cities, but operate in all of the nine provinces. Some of the larger casinos are part of large shopping complexes or have other attractions, including amusement parks, nearby.

South Africa also has a national lottery. It is known as The Lotto, for which winners are selected every Wednesday and Saturday.

60km (25 miles) east of Pretoria.
Cullinan Tourism
Tel: (012) 734 2665. Mine tours: Mon–Fri.

Lesedi Cultural Village

Xhosa, Zulu, Pedi and Basutho
homesteads have been built within the
village where visitors experience
something of the many traditional
cultures that make up South Africa.
Guides explain some of the intricacies of
each culture, and audiovisual displays
are also used.

Dancers later entertain tourists while
lunch is served. A variety of curios and
artwork is available as is overnight
accommodation.
*Call management for directions. About
45 minutes from Johannesburg and
25 minutes from Pretoria.
Tel: (012) 205-1394.
www.lesedi.com
Tours: daily 11.30am and 4.30pm.
Admission charge.*

Magaliesberg Mountains

Many residents of nearby Pretoria and
Johannesburg escape the cities on
weekends to enjoy outdoor pursuits in
the rolling countryside near the high
southerly facing cliffs of the
Magaliesberg mountains, which run for
some 100km east of Pretoria.

Many B&Bs and country lodges are
scattered throughout the region, and
innumerable stalls and shops offer crafts,
country food and other paraphernalia.

Horse riding, hiking, camping and
bird watching are just some of the
outdoor attractions which attract day-
trippers, although others simply visit the
area for a quiet weekend lunch and a bit
of casual shopping. The Magaliesberg
are easily accessible from both
Johannesburg and Pretoria.
Magaliesberg Tourism
*Tel: (012) 888 1154.
www.magaliesberg.co.za.*

Suikerbosrand Nature Reserve

High grass-covered hills and rocky
stream valleys give visitors an idea of
what the area around Johannesburg
would have looked like before the city
developed.

A surprising amount of small game
including antelope occurs in the 13,337-
hectare reserve, which is near the town
of Heidelberg some 45km from the
centre of Johannesburg. Hiking trails, a
circular drive and picnic sites have been
laid out in the hills.

Johannesburg and the surrounding
urban sprawl are visible from the
northern side of the reserve and provide
a sobering reminder of how much
humans have changed our planet.
*Tel: (011) 904 3930.
Open: all year.*

Copyright: South African Tourism

Hartebeespoort Dam

Soapstone elephant

KwaZulu-Natal

The 3,000m (9,750ft) high, sometimes snow-covered peaks of the uKhahlamba-Drakensberg mountains in KwaZulu-Natal slope steeply to sub-tropical, banana-tree-fringed beaches less than 200km to the east. Further north along the hot and humid coastline, Africa's southern-most coral reefs shelter a plethora of brightly coloured fish and other sealife. While only a few kilometres inland, the Big Five thrill tourists in some of Africa's oldest game reserves.

The North Coast, South Coast and Durban area itself offer good surfing, safe bathing and many exciting dive sites. Between the mountains and beaches, the rolling hills and grasslands of the Midlands and surrounding areas provide some of the best agricultural land in South Africa.

The geographical diversity of KwaZulu-Natal is matched by the cultural mix of its residents. Zulu, British and Indian traditions combine to create a vibrant mosaic of cuisine, dress and culture.

Ballito Beach in KwaZulu-Natal is warm all year round

KwaZulu-Natal, formerly known simply as Natal, was colonised by the British in the 19th century. The province later saw several wars fought between the settlers and the Zulu, and later the Boers (of Dutch descent).

Late in the 19th century, labourers were brought from India to work in the sugar-cane fields. Today, the province has the largest Indian community in the country. Zulu people make up the majority of the population and, accordingly, their influence in local government and culture is significant.

Many Zulu people live in rural areas and follow a traditional way of life but often move easily between city and country life.

DURBAN

Warm seas, broad beaches and easy access to the province's many attractions make Durban one of South Africa's most important holiday destinations. Over Christmas, the beaches are packed with holidaymakers, but the city's sub-tropical climate encourages tourists at any time of the year. In the middle of

Durban City Hall

what passes for winter, the city hosts one of the world's top surfing events. Winter daytime temperatures seldom fall below 21°C (70°F), and summer highs often exceed 30°C (86°F).

Culturally, Durban is a vibrant mix of African, Western and Indian cultures. Churches, mosques and synagogues rub shoulders with sidewalk stalls where traditional doctors sell medicines to cure ailments or to ward off evil spirits. As befitting a city with a large Indian population, Durban has become famous in South Africa as the home of hot, spicy curry dishes, but a cosmopolitan range of restaurants provides fare suitable for most palates. Shopping opportunities are nothing if not eclectic, and stores selling the latest electronic goods can be found next to noisy bazaars selling everything from shovels to chicken food.

Informal shops on the sidewalk in Durban

African Art Centre

Telephone-wire *imbenge* (baskets), beaded wooden or clay animals, ceramics, carvings and other items are made by Zulu and Xhosa women. It is well worth booking a lecture with one or more of the artists who will explain the cultural significance of beadwork and other items.
Tourist Junction, 160 Pine St.
Tel: (031) 304 7915.
Open: Mon–Fri 8.30–5pm, Sat 9am–1pm.

Coedmore Castle and Kenneth Stainbank Nature Reserve

Coedmore Castle was built by the Stainbank family in 1885 and today contains many of the original household contents which provide an interesting insight into colonial life. The castle is in the Kenneth Stainbank Nature Reserve, which protects an important remnant of the coastal forest that once covered much of the region.

A visit to the reserve shows what parts of Durban would have looked like 200 years ago. More than 300 species of birds and a relatively large number of mammals have been recorded here. Visitors can combine a visit to the castle with tea and a walk in the reserve. Many people pack a picnic to enjoy amongst the forest trees.

Coedmore Castle
Yellowwood Park. Tel: (031) 462 3005.
Call to book a visit. Admission charge.
Kenneth Stainbank Nature Reserve
Yellowwood Park. Tel: (031) 469 2807.
Open: 6am–6pm in summer,
6.30am–5.30pm in winter.
Small admission charge.

Durban City Hall, Durban Art Gallery and Natural Science Museum and Kwazuzukwazi Science Centre

The City Hall complex hosts civic functions and occasional symphony concerts. It also houses the Durban Art

Gallery and Natural Science Museum. The Art Gallery has several important displays including a comprehensive collection of Zulu beadwork, while the Natural Science Museum has good displays of animals and birds. Nearby, the Local History Museum and the Old House Museum explain Durban's colonial history. The City Hall was built in 1910, and is unusual in that it is a replica of the Belfast City Hall in Northern Ireland.

City Hall & Durban Art Gallery
Smith St. Tel: (031) 300 6911. Open: Mon–Sat 8.30am–5pm, Sun & public holidays 11am–5pm.

Natural Science Museum
Tel: (031) 311 2241. Same opening times as City Hall.

Old House Museum
St Andrews St. Tel: (031) 311 2261.

Open: Mon–Sat 8.30am–4pm, Sun & public holidays 11am–4pm.

Killie Campbell Collections
Set on the Berea Ridge overlooking the city, this museum is housed in Victorian-era Muckelneuk Mansion, the former home of sugar baron Sir Marshall Campbell. There is an extensive library of Africana books, manuscripts and maps.

It also contains an important collection of Zulu art, as well as displays of musical instruments, pottery, weapons and other items. The Berea also provides excellent view of Durban.
Corner Essenwood Rd and Marriot Rd. Tel: (031) 207 3432.
Viewing by appointment: Mon–Fri 8.30am–4.30pm.

Juma Mosque, Durban

Durban's popular 'Golden Mile' beachfront

Mosques and Hindu Temples

Durban has a rich variety of Muslim mosques and Hindu temples, and several have been declared national monuments. The Juma Mosque is the largest Muslim place of worship in South Africa, and is a well-known landmark. Its golden domes and ornate architecture form the heart of a busy and colourful shopping area dominated by Indian-owned stores. There are several Hindu temples across the city and its outskirts, and the Alayam Hindu Temple provides an excellent example of temple architecture.
Contact KwaZulu-Natal Tourism for a comprehensive list. Tel: (031) 366 7500. www.kzn.org.za

NSA Gallery

The NSA Gallery is situated among large old trees in Bulwer Park, and is divided into three exhibition areas, which provide a platform for the work of many young local artists. Exhibitions change often, so it is best to check the latest programmes. There is also a gift shop and restaurant.
Bulwer Road, Glenwood. Tel: (031) 202 3686/7/8. Open: Mon–Fri 9am–5pm, Sat 9am–4pm, Sun 10am–3pm. www.nsagallery.co.za

The Golden Mile

This 6km-stretch of beaches has for decades been the focal point of holidaymakers seeking safe swimming, good surfing and night-time entertainment. Fun fairs, shallow paddling pools and innumerable restaurants help entertain those tired of

DIVING

The KwaZulu-Natal south coast has some excellent diving sites. On the Aliwal Shoal, divers are treated to regular sightings of ragged-tooth sharks, fearsome in appearance, but docile in nature, moray eels and innumerable reef fish.

Large numbers of fish are also attracted to several wrecked ships, which act as artificial reefs. Further north, Umkomaas also offers good diving, and there are several other deeper sites suitable for experienced divers.

Contact KwaZulu-Natal Tourism for a comprehensive list of operators and other dive sites.
Tel: (031) 366 7500. www.kzn.org.za

the sun and sea.

Fringed by many high-rise hotels, the area is very busy on holidays and weekends. Visitors should be cautious of pickpockets and under no circumstances walk along back streets.

At the northern end of the Golden Mile is the Fitzsimmons Snake Park, which has a good collection of South African reptiles. At the southern end of the 'Mile', uShaka Marine World has an excellent aquarium and dolphinarium *(see entry below)*.

Fitzsimmons Snake Park

Tel: 073 156 9606.
Open: Mon–Sun 9.30am–4.30pm.
Demonstrations at regular intervals throughout the day.
Admission charge.

uShaka Marine World

The aquarium and dolphinarium provide an exiting and comprehensive insight into the sea-life of the warm waters of South Africa's east coast. Visitors can see sharks, turtles, dolphins and a wide variety of deep- and shallow-water fish, corals and seaweeds.

A Spice shop in Victoria Street, Durban

Displays include deep-water reefs and an interactive tidal pool where visitors are allowed to touch marine creatures and seaweeds. There is also a shipwreck reef. In this unique environment, you have the opportunity to snorkel with a huge variety of marine life.

There are freshwater displays focussing on the aquatic life encountered in KwaZulu-Natal's rivers and dams. Dolphin shows occur regularly, and water slides and a variety of other features provide entertainment for children.

Located at the southern end of Golden Mile. Tel: (031) 368 6675.
www.ushakamarineworld.co.za
Open: Mon–Fri 8am–5pm at time of writing, but will change. Call to confirm.

Victoria Street Market

This market is housed indoors but surrounded by innumerable shops and sidewalk stalls that stretch for several city blocks.

A wide array of goods is available within the market and everyone expects to bargain. Spices, fabrics, Indian jewellery, Zulu beadwork, elaborately decorated spears, carved masks and even fresh fish are available. In a morning,

Copyright: South African Tourism

Diving on the Aliwal Shoal, KwaZulu-Natal

ANGLING

Both saltwater and freshwater angling enthusiasts will find ample opportunity to pursue their hobby in South Africa. Whether fishing from the beach for shad or grunter or from a boat for marlin and sailfish, anglers will be spoilt for choice. Saltwater fly-fishing is also widely followed, and the kingfish test even the best anglers.

Freshwater fly-fishing for trout has a large following, but recently the hard-fighting indigenous yellowfish is luring more and more anglers. Licences are required for all types of fishing but are easily acquired.

visitors will meet an intriguing cross-section of Durban's residents.

Outside, street barbers offer quick haircuts to customers waiting for minibus taxis, while nearby vendors sell woven mats, clothing and live chickens.
Nearest corner: Queen St and Russell St.
Open: daily 6am–5pm.
Various tour operators.

Copyright: South African Tourism

The long coastline offers fine angling opportunities

Wilson's Wharf and The Point

Both these areas are close to the city centre and offer good harbour views. A variety of restaurants and pubs create a pleasant setting for lunchtime or evening meals.

Wilson's wharf overlooks a yacht marina and also has a good range of craft and curio shops. The Point is a great vantage point from which to watch vessels, ranging from small fishing boats to huge container ships, entering the port.
Wilson's Wharf
Boatman Street.
The Point
Off Point Road.
It is best to ask your hotel or tourist authorities for directions, and to arrange transport.

THE SOUTH COAST

The warm weather, laid-back attitude and good beaches make the South Coast a favourite holiday and retirement destination for many South Africans. This region runs for 160km (100 miles) south of Durban and, in addition to its beaches and seafood restaurants, has several crocodile farms, markets and good golf courses.

The Oribi Gorge Nature Reserve has about 35km of trails that wind in and out of a forested gorge, and fortunate visitors might spot some of the antelope and monkeys that live here.

The narrow-gauge Banana Express steam train runs from Port Shepstone to the Orbi Gorge Nature Reserve. The trip makes a good day outing, particularly for children.
For **Banana Express** *bookings call* **Port Shepstone Publicity.**

*Tel: (039) 682 4821. Call to
confirm schedule.*
Riverbend Croc Farm
*Tel: (039) 316 6204.
Open: Mon–Sun 9am–5pm.*

THE NORTH COAST

The North Coast has been heavily
developed in recent years with a string
of upmarket hotels and holiday
developments running for some 50km
(25 miles) north of Durban.

It is a good place for an easily
arranged stress-free holiday with plenty
of safe swimming beaches, good
restaurants and other entertainment.
Dolphins are often spotted along this
coast, hence its popular name of the
Dolphin Coast.
Dolphin Coast Publicity Association
Tel: (032) 946 1997.

Natal Sharks Board

Sharks are widely feared, but most
people's terror is based on
misconceptions. The Board offers
comprehensive audio-visual displays
and lectures, dispelling some of the
myths about these creatures which fill
an important ecological niche. Sharks
caught in the shark nets that protect
many beaches are sometimes dissected
during tours.

The board is situated at Umhlanga
Rocks some 20km (12 miles) north of
Durban. They monitor the shark nets
that protect many of KwaZulu-Natal's
bathing beaches, and boat tours can
be arranged.
Natal Sharks Board
*Tel: (031) 566 0400.
Open: Mon–Thurs and Sun with three*

Zulu man in traditional dress

Copyright: South African Tourism

*shows daily. Times vary so call for details.
Admission charge.*

Shakaland

Shakaland offers an 'interactive'
experience of life in a Zulu kraal a
hundred years ago. Zulu warriors with
shields and spears dance for guests,
storytellers recount tales of kings and
queens, and guides explain local
traditions. Overnight accommodation is
provided in traditional 'beehive huts'
made of grass woven over wooden poles.
Authentic traditional food including the
staple *phutu* (a stiff porridge made from
de-husked maize), and indigenous
vegetables are also available but
not compulsory.
*Shakaland is some 162km (101 miles)
north of Durban near the town of Eshowe.
Tel: (035) 460 0912 to arrange visits and
book accommodation.
Opens at 11am.
Admission charge.*

The spectacular game reserves of Zululand offer protection to a bewildering array of animals, birds, fish and plant life, and help make the region one of South Africa's top wildlife areas.

These reserves are some of the oldest in Africa. Hluhluwe Imfolozi Park was created as two separate parks in 1896, and has been the core of more than 100 years of pioneering conservation work, including the epic effort that saved the white rhino from extinction.

In the Greater St Lucia Wetlands Park, elephants and black rhinos browse within sight of hippos and crocodiles. A few kilometres away, the warm Indian Ocean nurtures coral reefs and prolific sea life including humpback whale passing by on the annual migration.

The lake, which is really an estuary and one of the largest in Africa, is surrounded by varying forms of forest, grasslands and woodlands. In addition to the elephants and rhinos, these areas support buffalo, leopard, zebra, reedbuck and many other species of mammal, as well as prolific birdlife.

High, forested sand dunes, among the highest in the world, roll down right to the edge of wide, sandy beaches. In summer, the beaches are used as nesting sites by logger-head turtles and huge leather-back turtles (really big specimens can weigh 600kg–1,320lb). The turtles lay their eggs towards the end of the year. Just over two months later, the babies make their first foray into the sea. Authorities run strictly

Copyright KZN Wildlife

controlled tours to watch both the nesting and hatching processes.

Various coral reefs fringe the shoreline, providing excellent snorkelling and diving.

There are several other parks along the coast including Kosi Bay and Mapelane. Kosi Bay is one of the most important estuary systems in the country, and is an important nursery for marine fish. There are also coral reefs at the mouth of the system, which comprises of four lakes of increasing salinity.

Further inland, neighbouring Mkhuze Game Reserve and the Phongola Biosphere Reserve offer protection to a wide range of species and habitat.

Not far away is Hluhluwe Imfolozi Park where conservationists managed to save the white rhino from possible extinction. These large, docile creatures had been hunted mercilessly until the 1920s, by which time their numbers had dwindled to a few dozen.

A few far-sighted conservationists pressed for a special programme to protect the white rhino, and also the black, and today South Africa is the stronghold of the world population. Worldwide some 11,000 white rhinos live in the wild and in zoos, but only about 3,300 black rhinos exist.

The area between the Black Umfolozi and White Umfolozi rivers was once the hunting ground of the Zulu King Shaka, and was off limits to commoners and outsiders. This restriction helped maintain the wildlife population before the first White settlers arrived.

Other protected areas include the mountainous Ithala Game Reserve and the Ndumo Game Reserve, which are two of the country's top birding spots with more than 400 species having been recorded. There are many privately run game reserves and lodges throughout the region, which also offer excellent accommodation and good game viewing.

Tel: (033) 845 1000.
ww.kznwildlife.com

Opposite: White rhino in the Hluhluwe Imfolosi Park, KwaZulu-Natal
Above: The sign is no joke. The Greater St Lucia Wetand Park has a large crocodile population

Elephants in the river, Hluhluwe Imfolozi Park

RESERVES AND PARKS
Hluhluwe Imfolozi Park
There is no easier place in the world to see rhinos in the wild. Around 1,200 white and 300 black rhino live in the park which constitutes one-tenth of the global population, and that's including those animals in captivity.

All the other members of the Big Five occur, as well as large populations of giraffe, nyala and other species. The Mpila and Hilltop camps offer accommodation ranging from self-catering in safari tents to upmarket, fully serviced lodges. There are also several 'bush lodges' which are set away from the main camps.

Short walks with skilled guides can be arranged and should not be missed. Longer three- and four-day trails, where walkers camp in the bush, are also on offer. Night drives can be booked and are another 'must do', as they enable visitors to see many nocturnal species that might otherwise be missed.

Greater St Lucia Wetland Park
This World Heritage site is actually an amalgamation of several reserves. It encompasses a wide range of habitats, including the huge Lake St Lucia beaches, coral reefs, grasslands and woodlands. Elephants, rhino, buffalo and antelope occur on the shores of the lake, and the reefs offer excellent diving and snorkelling. Bird life is exceptional. The beaches are broad and clean, and the water is warm nearly all year round. Accommodation ranges from comfortable lodges to camping, and many companies arrange tours. Sodwana Bay provides the easiest access points to the best coral reefs. There are self-catering chalets and privately run lodges and other accommodation nearby.

Ithala Game Reserve
Although less well known than some of the other parks, Ithala nevertheless is well worth visiting for its variety of habitat alone. The landscape is extremely rugged, and high mountains drop steeply down to the hot valley of the Phongola River.

Elephant, rhino and buffalo are regularly spotted, and the reserve is an excellent place to see the nocturnal aardwolf which, although it is as big as a medium-sized dog, lives on ants. The award-winning Ntshondwe Camp is built on the side of the Ngotshe mountains.

Ndumo and Mkhuze Game Reserves
Both the reserves offer excellent game viewing and are two of South Africa's premier birding sites. Ndumo is located on the border of Mozambique, and its

many pans (small natural lakes), fringed with the yellow-barked fever trees, create a sense of tropical Africa. Thick forest and dense reed beds add to the atmosphere of adventure.

Although neither reserve is very large, they are both enormously diverse. *Parks open all year round.*
Contact **Ezemvelo KZN Wildlife**
Tel: (033) 845 1000.
www. kznwildlife.com
Contact **KZN Tourism** *for a comprehensive list of private reserves and lodges.*
Tel: (031) 366 7500.
www.kzn.org.za

The uKhahlamba-Drakensberg Park

This 250,000-hectare (600,000-acre) Park is also a World Heritage Site, and throughout the mountain range sheer cliffs, steep sandstone-fringed foothills and cold, clear streams create a peaceful world far removed from the hustle and bustle of cities.

Summers are warm with regular thunderstorms. Winters can be icy with occasional snowfalls, and many high-altitude streams freeze at night. Peaks here average over 3,000m (9,750ft).

The entire range offers excellent hiking, walks, horse riding and birding. Large game is scarce at high altitude but many small species do occur. The rare bearded vulture is often seen as are black eagles, lanner falcons and a host of smaller birds.

These mountains proved to be one of the last refuges of the San (Bushman). Hundreds of their rock paintings and engravings can be found in the caves and rock shelters of the foothills known

Champagne Castle, uKhahlamba-Drakensberg mountains

Copyright: South African Tourism

as the 'Little Berg'.

There are plenty of hotels, B&Bs and guest farms dotted along the entire length of the mountain range, and these offer a wide range of activities including tennis, fly-fishing, mountain-bike riding, abseiling and other sports. The Park is comprised of many smaller reserves including those listed below.

Didima (Cathedral Peak)

Didima offers the best of both worlds – the outdoor splendour of the mountains and the luxurious comfort of imaginatively designed chalets and restaurant.

There is a comprehensive San art interpretive centre where the long, and sometimes sad, history of the San is explained. The display also explains the spiritual role art played in the life of these nomadic hunters.

For the fit, there are day hikes to the top of Cathedral Peak. Many easier walks are, however, accessible, and if the going gets too hot, a plunge into a mountain pool is likely to invigorate most hikers.

Giant's Castle accommodation

Giant's Castle

Set above the clear Bushman's River, the main rest camp has spectacular views of the high, blue-grey walls and peaks of the uKhahlamba-Drakensberg (*uKhahlamba* means 'barrier of spears' in Zulu and *Drakensberg* means 'dragon mountain' in Afrikaans).

The San once hunted eland and other animals in the deep valleys beneath 'the Giant'. Hundreds of their rock paintings and engravings can be found in many caves and rock shelters in the area. One of the best collections is at the main caves just a short walk from the comfortable main camp.

Visitors spend time hiking, horse riding, trout fishing or simply relaxing at the edge of a mountain stream or in the quiet gardens of the rest camp itself. Injisuthi camp, further north, offers self-catering chalets and tents in a remote valley surrounded by sandstone cliffs.

Royal Natal and Rugged Glen

The breathtaking 5km- (3 mile-) long sheer wall of the Amphitheatre is the focal point of Royal Natal. The Thukela River starts life high on the summit before tumbling down sheer cliffs to

Winter scene, Giant's Castle

The rolling sugar-cane fields and plantations of the KwaZulu-Natal Midlands

form one of the highest waterfalls in the world.

Royal Natal offers the tranquillity found throughout the 'Berg' and is one of South Africa's most popular mountain destinations. Hikes and walks ranging from a few hours to several days can be undertaken along well-marked paths, and trout fishing and horse riding are also very popular.

Elsewhere in the Berg

There are other provincial parks including the Coleford, Kamberg and Loteni nature reserves, as well as dozens of private hotels, guest farms and B&Bs.

The Giant's Cup and Mkhomazi Wilderness Areas offer exhilarating hiking along the face of the mountains, with overnight stops in caves or mountain huts. These hikes are for the fit only, but well worth the time and effort.

Parks open all year round.

Contact **Ezemvelo KZN Wildlife**
Tel: (033) 845 1011.

No need to worry – the Cannibal Cave hiking trail is great fun

The Valley of a Thousand Hills near Dunbar

www. kznwildlife.com
*Contact **KZN Tourism** for a list of*
private lodges, B&Bs, campsites and tours.
Tel: (031) 366 7500.
www.kzn.org.za

THE MIDLANDS

Set among the lush green hills, the
Midlands Meander arts and craft route
runs through some of KwaZulu-Natal's
most beautiful scenery. More than 160
craft shops, art galleries, restaurants,
hotels, and B&Bs are scattered along
country roads beginning about 25km
(155 miles) north of Pietermaritzburg.

The area is ideal for weekends spent
wandering along, while shopping and
stopping for tea, lunch or dinner.
Just outside the town of Howick, the
Umgeni River tumbles over the 95m-
high Howick Falls. At nearby Midmar
Dam and the surrounding nature
reserve there is an historical village and
open-air museum. The area offers good
water sports, riding and game viewing.

It is best to visit the Meander website
or to get a copy of their extensive
brochure to plan your trip according to
your tastes.

Midlands Meander Association
Tel: (033) 330 8195.
www.midlandsmeander.co.za

PIETERMARITZBURG

This sleepy city is the capital of the
province, and was established by the
Boer Voorterkkers fleeing British rule in
1838. The British took over the city in
1843, and it became the capital of the
Colony of Natal. The city still has many
buildings dating from the 19th century,
including the all-brick City Hall, the Old
Natal Parliament and the Railway
Station. Seventy of these buildings are
national monuments, and self-guided
trails enable visitors to see many of
them in a few hours walk.

Carpets for sale in the Midlands

The annual Comrades Marathon is run between Durban and Pietermaritzburg

The Voortrekker Museum housed in the small gabled Church of the Vow was erected in 1841 by the Boers. It commemorates the Battle of Blood River, and depicts life during that time. The nearby Natal Museum is devoted to the region's social and natural history. The Tatham Art Gallery contains European and South African works, and there are also a number of interesting churches, mosques and Hindu temples in the city.

GANDHI

Pietermaritzburg played an ungracious but important role in the early life of Indian pacifist, Mohandas Gandhi (later known as Mahatma). In 1893, he was evicted from the first-class carriage of a train at Pietermaritzburg Station because of his race. He later said the incident triggered his philosophy of passive resistance based on truth and compassion.

Gandhi became an international symbol of passive resistance, and a statue in his memory was erected outside the Old Colonial Building in 1993.

Pietermaritzburg Tourism
177 Long St. Tel: (033) 345 1348.
www.pmbtourism.co.za
Tatham Art Gallery
Tel: (033) 342 1804.
Open: Tues–Sun 10am–6pm.
Voortrekker Museum
333 Boom St. Tel: (033) 394 6834. Open: Mon–Fri 9am–4pm, Sat 9am–1pm.
Natal Museum
237 Loop St.
Tel: (033) 345 1404. Open: Mon–Fri 9am–4.30pm, Sat 10am–4pm, Sun 11am–3pm.

Tour: KwaZulu-Natal Battlefields

Some of the fiercest battles ever fought in South Africa raged across the hills and valleys of KwaZulu-Natal throughout the 19th century, leaving thousands of dead Zulu, British and Boer soldiers, women and children.

Allow two days. Start at Spioenkop, which is about 150km (94 miles) north of Pietermartizburg on the N3 freeway. At the N11 junction turn left to Spioenkop which is about 18km (12 miles) west of the freeway. Retrace your route to the N3, and Ladysmith is a further 14km (8 miles) to the east along the N11.

Battle displays at Rorke's Museum

Early Boer settlers clashed several times with Zulu armies in the late 1830s. In 1879, the ferocious Anglo-Zulu War erupted. During the South African War (Anglo-Boer War) of 1899–1902, some of the worst fighting took place in KwaZulu-Natal. Dozens of other battles also took place.

1 Siege of Ladysmith

In one of the most famous battles of the South African War, Boer commandos surrounded British forces in Ladysmith and kept them trapped there for 118 days. The water supply ran out, food shortages became acute and disease broke out, killing many in the town. Both defenders and attackers took heavy casualties in the fighting until the town was relieved on 28 February 1900.

2 Spioenkop

Earlier British forces sent to relieve Ladysmith fought a bitter battle against the Boers for the strategic mountain of Spioenkop which overlooks Ladysmith. *Spioenkop walk and tape tours available. Tel: (036) 488 1578. Open: daily 6am–6pm.*

Ladysmith Siege Museum
Tel: (036) 637 2992. Open: Mon–Fri 9am–4pm, Sat 9am–1pm.

From Ladysmith take the N11 north for about 75km (47 miles) until the junction with the R68 to Dundee. Follow the R68 for 22km (13 miles). The battlefield is on the eastern side of the town.

3 Talana Battlefield

This was the scene of the first battle between the British and Boers in 1899. The Boers won the battle, and the British retreated to Ladysmith where they were later trapped. Graves and monuments mark the site of the battle.

British graves at the Talana Hill battlesite, KwaZulu-Natal

Copyright: South African Tourism

Isandhlwana, the site of a famous Zulu victory over the British

There is also a museum that documents Dundee's history as a coal mining and glass-manufacturing town.

Talana Museum
Tel: (034) 212 2654.
Choice of guided and self-guided tours of battlefield.
www.talana.co.za

Dundee Tourism
Tel: (034) 212 212. Open: Mon–Fri 8am–4.30pm. Sat, Sun & public holidays 10am–4pm. Closed: Christmas Day.

It is about 45km (28 miles) from Dundee to Rorke's Drift on the R68. Follow the signs to Isandhlwana which is about 30km (18 miles) further.

4 Isandhlwana and Rorke's Drift

On 22 January 1879 the Zulu Army, although later vanquished, inflicted the largest ever defeat of the British colonial army at Isandhlwana. More than 870 British soldiers were killed.

Several Zulu regiments then moved on to attack Rorke's Drift where a small number of men fought vastly superior forces for more than 12 hours. Eleven of the defenders later received the Victoria Cross, Britain's highest award for bravery.

There is a good arts and crafts centre over the road from the museum.
Isandhlwana Battle site enquiries.
Tel: (034) 271 0634.
Open: all week, but call first.

Rorke's Drift Museum
Tel: (034) 642 1687.
Open: all week, but call first.

From Rorke's Drift, follow the road back to the R68, and then head towards the R33 and Dundee. The Blood River turnoff is 27km (16 miles) east of Dundee on the R33, and the battlefield a further 20km southeast.

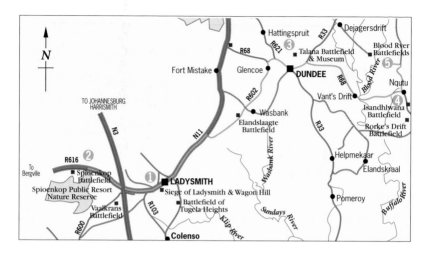

5 Blood River/Ncome

This battle forms one of the cornerstones of Afrikaner history. Today the 1838 battlefield is a hallowed spot for some Afrikaners, who believe that their God supported them in defeating the Zulus.

The battle was the result of an attempt to punish the Zulus for what the Voortrekkers believed to be the murder of one of their leaders. A small Voortrekker party took on a far superior Zulu force and won. There is a replica *laager* (circle) of 68 wagons commemorating the Boer victory, and also a monument to the Zulu soldiers who died.

Ncome Museum
Tel: (034) 271 8121.
Open: Mon–Sun 8am–4pm.

The Museum at Rorke's Drift, KwaZulu-Natal

Tour: Old Zulu Kingdom

Old Zululand covered a vast tract of central KwaZulu-Natal. One of the most interesting sections lies north of Durban, particularly between the Tugela River and the Swazi border. Here there are Zulu homesteads, historic battlegrounds, memorials and forts.

Allow at least 2 days. Start at Stanger and drive up the N2 for 56km to Gingindlovu.

Zulu dancers

1 Gingindlovu

Gingindlovu 'swallower of the elephant' was the site of a military *kraal* (settlement) built by Cetshwayo (Shaka's nephew) to commemorate victory over his brother, Mbulazi, in their contest for the Zulu throne. The *kraal* was destroyed by the British in 1879.
From Gingindlovu, take the R66 to Eshowe (26km).

2 Eshowe

Eshowe (sound of wind in the trees) was a quiet summer retreat for the Zulus.

Zulu crafts

Shaka's Kraal overlooks the nearby Nkwalini Valley. Cetshwayo's first kraal was here in 1860, before he moved to Ulundi. It was replaced by the British-built Fort Nongqai (1883), now the Zululand Historical Museum. Near Eshowe Nkandla Forest Reserve (place of exhaustion) is the grave of Cetshwayo who died in 1884.
For Shaka's Kraal, take the R68 north from Eshowe (6km), right on the R230 (dirt road) for about 20km. Continue along the R68 to Melmoth (27km), then turn onto the R34 and continue for 24km to uMgungundhlovu.

3 uMgungundlovu

Dingane moved the Zulu capital from KwaDukuza to uMgungundlovu (place of the great elephant), where Voortrekker leader Piet Retief and his men were executed in February 1838. Retribution was grim: 3,000 warriors were killed at the Battle of Blood River (see p81).

The uMgungundlovu Museum occupies the site of the *kraal*, the core of which has been accurately rebuilt.
Take the R66 to Ulundi (about 18km).

4 Ulundi

It was customary for a newly crowned king to establish his own capital: Ulundi was Cetshwayo's (1873). The British destroyed it in 1879, finally breaking Zulu military power. A second capital at Ondini (the heights) was burned by the Swazis. The local government rebuilt it as the KwaZulu Cultural Museum, and the royal quarters have been re-created. Close to Ulundi, is the eMakhosini Valley and royal burial ground. From Ulundi, the route branches east, passing through the Hluhluwe Imfolozi Park

(see p72).

Leave the park on the R618 access road and, at the junction with the N2, head south and back via Stanger to Durban.

Fort Nonqai

Nonqai Road.
Tel: (035) 474 4976. Open: Mon–Sat 9am–4pm.

KwaZulu Cultural Museum

3km east of town at Ondini.
Tel: (035) 870 2050. www.heritage.co.za
Open: Mon–Fri 9.30am–5pm.
Admission charge for both museums.

Limpopo

Most people in this province derive their livelihoods from agriculture and the wildlife industry. The northern half of the Kruger National Park is in Limpopo, but there are many smaller reserves and private game ranches scattered throughout the province. Many of the ranches cater for the hunting industry which attracts many foreign clients. Every Easter, more than a million pilgrims visit the Zionist Christian Church headquarters at Moria, near the capital city Polokwane.

Tzaneen and Magoebaskloof

The cold trout streams of the Magoebaskloof Pass drop steeply down to the sub-tropical mango, avocado pear and litchi farms around Tzaneen.

Tzaneen is in a transition zone between the hot Lowveld and cooler Highveld.

The game ranches that border the Kruger National Park begin east of Tzaneen, and to the northeast is the

Ndebele pots

The fertile Magoebaskloof valley

Modjadji Forest, home to the huge Modjadji palm, a form of cycad which evolved over 50 million years ago and grows to a height of some 13m (42ft). The area is also home to the Modjaji Rain Queen, a descendant of a 16th century Karanga princess, who is reputed to know the secrets of making rain. People still consult the Queen and ply her with gifts to bring good rains.

Soutpansberg

In the far north of the Limpopo Province, the Soutpansberg mountains form an enormously biologically diverse zone. The southern slopes of the mountains are among some of the wettest in South Africa. The northern slopes are however dry, and soon give way to the plains and the giant baobab trees that are so characteristic of the Limpopo River Valley.

There are many private game lodges and reserves in the mountains and on the surrounding plains. Hiking trails and game viewing dominate activities in this area, which is also an important tropical fruit-farming region.

The region is also the home of the Venda people who settled here in the 18th century. Many sites in the area are sacred. At Dsatza are ruins of ancient stone structures, and Lake Fundudzi is believed to be the home of a python god.

NDEBELE ART

Their extraordinary art is the single aspect of South Ndebele culture that distinguishes it from that of other Nguni groups. Usually referred to simply as Ndebele, the South Ndebele live for the most part in the Limpopo Highveld, northeast of Pretoria.

From house painting to beadwork, mural painting to the elaborate traditional dress style of the women, the Ndebele's striking attention to colour and pattern and their sense of symmetry are unusual. The palette of the original Ndebele house painters was restricted to ochre, natural clays and charcoals. Their beadwork has considerable cultural significance. Specific designs and garments are reserved for, as an example, married women, and others for widows.

The baobab tree, a resident of the hot north

Mpumalanga

The Kruger National Park is Mpumalanga's most famous attraction, but the province also has some of the best trout fishing in South Africa, many smaller game parks and wonderful scenery. Just over 120 years ago, the hills around Barberton and Pilgrim's Rest were the focus of a frenzied gold rush. Museums in many towns exhibit memories of the South African War (1899–1902). Shangaan culture is also highlighted in several art galleries and cultural villages.

Barberton

Barberton was founded after the discovery of gold. Its fame, however, was short lived, as the far richer finds on the Witwatersrand caused an almost immediate exodus of fortune seekers. Many of the town's old buildings survived, including the Kaap Gold Fields' Stock Exchange, the Transvaal's first stock exchange, and the 1887 Globe Tavern, a hostelry of a type common in the goldfields of the late 19th century.

The Barberton Museum contains artefacts relating to the gold rush days. In Barberton Park there is a statue of the dog Jock, the subject of Sir Percy FitzPatrick's famous story, *Jock of the Bushveld*. Many people hike or ride horses in the hills around Barberton.
Barberton Information Bureau
Tel: (013) 712 2121.

Dullstroom

Dullstroom has become a trendy weekend getaway destination, and is the centre of the thriving trout fishing industry. Many people visit the area to simply walk in the hills and to spend a quiet weekend at one of the wide range of guest farms or lodges. Others pursue the brown and rainbow trout with passion. A wide range of craft shops and restaurants have been established in the village and surrounding areas.

Nearby Lydenberg is also an important fly-fishing area.
Dullstroom Accommodation
Tel: (013) 254 0234.
www.dullstroom.co.za

Copyright: South African Tourism

Barberton in Mpumalanga

Hazyview
Shangaan Cultural Village
Dressed in traditional skins and headdresses, Shangaan dancers and storytellers recount some of the legends of their people and region at this village close to the borders of the Kruger National Park. Curios made by local people are also sold at The Marula Market in the village.
Hazyview.
Tel: (013) 737 7000.
www.shangana.co.za
Open: daily, but contact them for performance times.

Nelspruit and White River
Nelspruit is the largest town and capital of Mpumalanga. It is also the gateway to the Lowveld.

The Lowveld National Botanical Gardens are well worth visiting, and have an impressive collection of cycads. Other Lowveld flowers and trees are well represented.

Nearby is the sub-tropical town of White River where mangos, avocados and other fruit are gown. Soon after White River, the orchards begin to make way for game-ranching land.
Lowveld National Botanical Gardens
Tel: (013) 752 5531.
www.nbi.ac.za

Sudwala Caves
West of Nelspruit on the slopes of the Northern Drakensberg are the Sudwala Caves. Visitors are only allowed to pass through the first few hundred metres, and the total depth of the cavern system is still uncertain.

Within the cave are bizarre rock formations, spectacular stalactites and stalagmites and fossils of prehistoric algae. Below the entrance to the caves there is a restaurant and an open-air museum with some life-size replicas of dinosaurs and other prehistoric creatures.

Mpumalanga Tourism Authority
Tel: (013) 752 7001.
www.mpumalanga.com

Pilgrim's Rest

Kruger National Park

Sprawling across a vast expanse of hot, game-rich bush and woodland cut by four major rivers and bordered by two others is the Kruger National Park. The Park is one of Africa's premier wildlife areas and tourist destinations. The Park covers some 20,000sq km, and there are 25 camps offering many types of accommodation.

There are several top-of-the-range, privately run lodges too. Each rest camp offers something different in the way of scenery, and the game and birdlife varies according to habitat.

The view from the Olifants thatched camp, high on the hill overlooking the Olifants River, is spectacular. Visitors get eye-level views of circling marabou storks and vultures, while far below elephants browse among the knob thorn and mopane trees.

Further south near Skukuza, the largest camp in the park, wild dogs are often spotted, and lucky visitors sometimes see these rare predators hunting, their white tipped tails streaming behind them as they chase their quarry through the bush. Almost 500 species of bird occur in the park.

Many species of mammals, reptiles, trees and even insects keep hefty guidebooks busy.

The area covered by Kruger also has a rich human history. Near Pafuri, the stone citadel of Thulamela, which has now been restored to its former glory, dates back to the Late Iron Age. It was an important cultural and trading settlement with links to other stone cities like Great Zimbabwe. A vital component in southern African, and worldwide, conservation, Kruger attracts more than a million visitors a year.

Recently, fences between the Kruger National Park and a conservation area in neighbouring Mozambique have been taken down, enabling the formation of the Great Limpopo Transfrontier Park. Similarly, fences have been taken down along the western boundary of the Kruger National Park. This allows the free movement of game from well-run, upmarket private game reserves developed along the Park's boundary.

Kruger Tips:

- If you are on a self-drive trip in the Kruger National Park, plan your day carefully. Distances are considerable, and game viewing takes time.
- All camp gates are locked at last light and only opened again at daybreak.
- The speed limit on tar roads is 50kph (30mph), and on gravel roads it is 40kph (25mph). Authorities set up speed traps and issue fines in an attempt to control speeding. Cars kill hundreds of wild animals and birds annually.
- In summer, it is best to get up at first-light and travel in the cool of the morning. Return to camp for a brunch, and siesta in the middle of the day when the temperatures can climb dramatically. Go out on another game drive after 3pm.
- Make sure to book a night drive with a trained guide – private individuals are not allowed to drive outside the camps at night.
- Talk to other guests and park staff about game sightings. It will help you plan your viewing, although there is no guarantee that the animals will be in the same place.
- Take adequate supplies of food and drink with you when you set off on a drive.

Opposite top: Pretoriuskop Camp in the Kruger
Opposite bottom: The magnificent bateleur eagle is common in Kruger National Park
Below: A lion cub

The 'Big Five' are the trump cards of African game reserves. Everyone wants to see them. The 'Big Five' are the elephant, lion, buffalo, leopard and rhino. The term has an unfortunate origin – to early hunters these were considered to be the most dangerous animals to kill, and in some instances the hunters did become the hunted with fatal consequences.

Today these animals are considered hugely important in the tourism industry, and have status that would have shocked people 100 years ago. In many instances they were considered to be, at best, pests and, in some instances, vermin.

The Big Five

Lion

Research shows that tourists like to watch these animals more than any other species. They are the only communal large cats and live in prides that sometimes exceed 20 animals. Large males weigh over 200kg (440lb) and females average around 130kg

Copyright: South African Tourism

(286lb). They often hunt co-operatively, some animals flushing prey and others making the kill.

Popular myth has it that males simply eat whatever lionesses kill, but the reality is that they are fearsome predators and often kill for themselves. They usually hunt under cover of darkness.

Elephant

Elephants are the second most-popular animals amongst visitors to Africa. Male elephants are huge, and some mature bulls weigh over 6,500kg (14,300lb) and

Copyright: South African Tourism

stand about 3,3m (10ft9in) at the shoulder. Females are considerably smaller.

They are entirely vegetarian and eat leaves, fruit, bark, grass and other vegetable matter. They have a considerable impact on their environment due to their habit of pushing over trees to get at succulent new leaves and twigs. Female matriarchs lead all herds, but mature bulls visit regularly to mate.

Rhinoceros

Two species, the black and the white, occur in southern Africa. The white rhino is the larger of the two, bulls weigh up to 2,600kg (5,760lb), whereas the black rhino seldom weighs more than 1,200kg (2,640lb). The black rhino has a reputation for being bad tempered and charging without warning, but they usually only do so when they feel threatened.

The black rhino (photo below) is endangered, with only about 3,300 individuals left in the wild and captivity worldwide.

Leopard

Leopards are usually secretive animals and sometimes live close to human settlements for years without being detected. These solitary carnivores are remarkably strong for their size. Males weigh about 80–90kg (176–198lb), and hunt by sight and hearing. They are quite capable of killing animals much larger than themselves.

Leopards are exceptionally patient hunters and will spend long periods crouching motionless while watching their prey. These spotted cats are extremely beautiful, and once seen in the wild are seldom forgotten.

African Buffalo

Although they may look like large, docile cows, buffalo can be extremely aggressive and often drive off lions attacking a herd member. Lone bulls are notoriously short-tempered, and walking through thick bush when they are around can be a nerve-wracking experience.

They weigh between 700–800kg (1,540–1,760lb).

Tour: Northern Drakensberg Mountains

This tour winds through the Northern Drakensberg mountains, and takes in a series of spectacular vistas of the mountains and the Lowveld far below. Along the way, there are many opportunities to stop for a snack or shop.

The tour is suitable for a self-drive trip, although several companies offer tours that follow a similar route.

Allow a full day. Start at Sabie, and head north past Graskop along the edge of the escarpment on the R37, and then along the R532 to the Blyde River Canyon.

Eccentric carvings at the roadside near Ohrigstad

1 Sabie and Graskop

The pleasant village of Sabie is the centre of a thriving commercial forestry industry. There are several high

An old miner's house, which is now a shop, in Pilgrim's Rest

Lisbon Falls near Graskop

to Graskop.

The Forestry Museum in Sabie tells the story of the industry in the area. Graskop, 29km (18 miles) to the north was once a gold-mining settlement, but is today also closely linked to the forestry industry and tourism. Be sure to stop and enjoy the magnificent view of the Blyde River Canyon from the God's Window view site near Graskop. *Beyond God's Window, the R532 continues past the Bourke's Luck Potholes, which have been ground into the rock by the swirling waters. There are viewing platforms here. The road continues to the Blydepoort Nature Reserve.*

waterfalls in the area including the Bridal Veil Falls (70m/230ft), the Lone Creek Falls (68m/223ft) and the Mac Mac Falls (64m/210ft) on the way

2 Blyde River Canyon and Blydepoort Nature Reserve

The Blyde River gouges its way through the mountains, and has created a 20km-long canyon that is 800m deep in places.

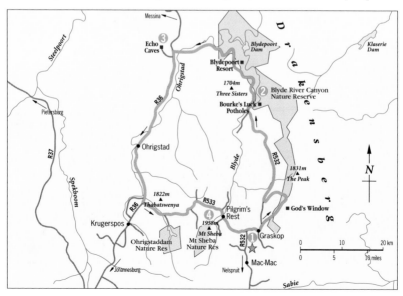

There are any number of panoramic views here, and dominating the area are three peaks known as the Three Sisters (also known as the Three Rondavels). The Lisbon and Berlin falls are nearby.

The area around the dam that has been created in the canyon is a nature reserve, and there is a wide variety of hiking trails that wind along the face of the mountains. There is accommodation to suit all tastes throughout the area. *From Blydepoort the road heads north to the junction of the R36. Turn left here onto the R36 towards Ohrigstad. Close to the junction is the road to the Echo Caves.*

3 Echo Caves

The sequence of chambers in the Molopong Valley has yielded a rich collection of Middle and Late Stone Age implements. There is an open-air display of archaeological implements. *Follow the R36 to Ohrigstad and then take the R533 to Pilgrim's Rest.*

4 Pilgrim's Rest

This entire village has been declared a national monument. It was the scene of a gold rush after Alec 'Wheelbarrow' Patterson found alluvial deposits of the

Dustbin at the God's window view site

precious metal here in 1887. Much of the town has been preserved in its original state, and the main road is lined with red and white corrugated-iron buildings.

The post-office building and other museums house memorabilia of the gold-rush era. Many of the stores in the town sell curios and artwork.
Pilgrim's Rest Tourist Information
Tel: (013) 768 1471.
Continue on the R533 until it joins the R534 back to Graskop.

Roadside hawker selling his zebras

ROADSIDE HAWKERS

In many parts of South Africa hawkers sell curios and other goods at the roadside. Many offer prices much lower than established shops. It is, however, wise to check wooden carvings, especially the larger items, for cracks or splits. In some cases, shoe polish is used to hide the cracks.

Many of the carvings, particularly those of giraffes, are designed to stand, but check the bases to make sure they are flat. In some cases they may seem perfectly okay at the roadside but are, in reality, craftily supported with stones or sticks.

The Three Rondavels (huts) in the Blydepoort Nature Reserve

North West

The Pilanesberg and Madikwe Game Reserves and the Sun City golf course and entertainment complex are the tourism hubs of this rural province. All three destinations are close enough to Johannesburg and Pretoria for quick visits. Both game reserves are relatively small and have thriving populations of the Big Five and other animals, which usually ensures good game viewing. Platinum mining, farming and tourism are the major economic activities of the province.

Pilanesberg National Park

Situated around the remains of an ancient volcano, this park provides the closest Big Five game viewing to Johannesburg, which is just two hours away by road.

The reserve was formed with the purchase of cattle farms in the 1970s and restocked with wild game, one of the largest operations of it kind ever undertaken. A network of good roads and large animal populations usually

Game Viewing Hide, Mankwe Dam, Pilanesberg National Park

ensure good game viewing. A wide range of accommodation is available. Weekends have become very busy, because the reserve is so close to Johannesburg and Pretoria.

Pilanesberg National Park
170km west of Johannesburg.
Tel: (014) 555 5351.
Open: all year round.

Sun City

This complex of hotels, casinos and golf courses is South Africa's answer to Las Vegas. The expensive Lost City complex is a fantasyland of carved animals and an opulent, palace-like hotel. The older Sun City has similar, if less grand, facilities and the Valley of the Waves water attraction provides a seaside experience, complete with artificially generated breakers, for children hundreds of kilometres from the nearest ocean.

Both complexes have world-class golf courses, and in December some of the world best players compete here for a vast amount of prize money.

Lost City complex

The complex is on the borders of the Pilanesberg National Park.
Sun City
Tel: (011) 780 7800.

The Waterberg

For decades, most tourists, including South Africans, ignored this rugged region. However, with the development of a new national park and a whole range of private game reserves, it is starting to get the attention it deserves.

Although the Marakele National Park is still in the early stages of development, it shares a boundary with the Welgevonden complex of private game reserves. Together the two form a malaria-free Big Five wildlife area with good game viewing.

Further north, the Lapalala Wilderness has established itself as an excellently run private reserve, and the Touchstone Ranch offers horseback safari amongst wild game.
Waterberg Tourism Association
Tel: (014) 755 3535.
www.waterbergtourism.com

Madikwe Game Reserve

This is another game reserve that was formerly cattle farms, that has been restocked with game including the Big Five. It is also malaria free. Although self-drive visits are not allowed, there are several lodges in the reserve, and all offer day and night drives with trained guides.

The area is hot in summer and has mild winter days.
Madikwe Game Reserve
Tel: (018) 3672 and ask for 2411, or view the following websites:
Etali Safari Lodge
http://www.etalisafari.co.za
Jaci's Safari Lodge
http://www.madikwe.com
The Bush House
http://www.madikwehouse.co.za
Madikwe River Lodge
http://www.country-escapes.co.za/madik.htm
Mateya Safari Lodge
http://www.mateyasafari.co.za
Mosetlha Bush Camp
http://www.thebushcamp.com
Tau Game Lodge
http://www.taugamelodge.co.za

18th hole at Sun City golf course

Northern Cape

The Northern Cape is South Africa's most sparsely populated province, and shares remote borders with Nambia and Botswana. The province is primarily a sheep and cattle farming region, although Kimberley, the largest city, owes its existence to the rich deposits of diamonds first found there over 130 years ago. Near Kimberley are the important South African War battle sites of Modder River and Magersfontein. The huge Kgalagadi Transfrontier Park to the north is a premier tourist destination.

Kimberley

In July 1871, the first diamonds were discovered at Colesberg Kopje (a *kopje* is a small hill), around which Kimberley, initially a tent-town of fortune seekers, sprung up.

The entire hill was dug away as miners found more and more diamonds. In later years even more miners continued digging straight down until they had created Kimberley's famous 'Big Hole', which is 800m (2,624ft) deep. More than 14 million carats of diamonds were extracted.

Today, it is part of an open museum, which incorporates entire streets of turn-of-the-century buildings. The Boers besieged the city during the South African War, but many of the old buildings have been preserved. There are several other good museums and art galleries in the city. One of these is the Sol Plaatjie House, which houses displays detailing the lives of Black people during the War and in later years. Plaatjie was one of the founders of the African National Congress. The William Humphreys Art Gallery and the Duggan-Cronin Gallery contain important South African and international art works. The McGregor Museum details the cultural and natural history of the region. Underground mine tours are conducted near the Bultfontein Mine.

Kimberley Publicity Association
Tel: (053) 832 7298.
www.kimberley.org.za

The Big Hole, Kimberley was one of the richest sources of diamonds ever found

Copyright: South African Tourism

Kimberley Mine Museum

Sol Plaatjie House
Angle Street. Tel: 082 804 3266.
Viewing by appointment Mon–Fri
8am–5pm.
Admission charge.

McGregor Museum
1 Atlas Road.
Tel: (053) 839 2700.
Open: Mon–Sat 9am–5pm, Sun
2pm–5pm, public holidays 10am–5pm.
Admission charge.

Duggan-Cronin Gallery
Egerton Rd.
Tel: (053) 833 2645.
Opening times as for the McGregor
Museum but closed between 1pm–2pm.
Donation.

Kimberley Mine Museum and Big Hole
Tucker St.
Tel: (053) 833 1557.
Open: daily 8am–6pm. Closed: Christmas
Day, Good Friday.
Admission charge.

William Humphreys Art Gallery
Cullinan Crescent. Tel: (053) 831 1724.

The Augrabies Falls on the Orange River

Kgalagadi Transfrontier National Park

Open: Mon–Sat 10am–1pm & 2pm–5pm. Sun 2pm–5pm. Admission charge.
Underground Mine Tours
Opposite the Bultfontein and Dutoitspan Mines. Tel: (053) 842 1321. Open: Mon, Tue, Thurs & Fri 8am–4.30pm. Booking necessary and no children under 16 allowed.
Wildebeest Rock Art Centre
Barclay West Rd.
Tel: (053) 833 7069.
Open: Mon–Fri 10am–5pm, Sat & Sun 11am–4pm. Admission charge.

Near Kimberley

The battles of Magersfontein and Modder River were fought in 1899 during the South African War and its campaign to relieve Kimberley. Magersfontein was one of the worst British defeats of the war, but there were many clashes in the area, not least the Siege of Kimberley, which lasted 124 days.

There is a small museum at the Magersfontein battle site.
The **Magersfontein battle site** *is 32km from Kimberley on the Modder Road. Open: daily 8am–5pm. Closed: Christmas Day & Good Friday.*

Augrabies Falls National Park

Although they are far off the beaten track, these falls are worth visiting if travelling to the Kgalagadi Transfrontier Park. The broad Orange River dominates life in the arid Northern Cape and is the focal point of the 18,000-hectare Augrabies Falls National Park. Here the river is channelled into an 18km ravine, which becomes a maelstrom of thundering white water and spray as it crashes over ledges 56m

(184ft) and 35m (115ft) high.

The falls are among the largest in the world. The park protects many desert and semi-desert plant species as well as antelope, including the gemsbok and springbok.

SA National Parks Central Reservations
Tel: (012) 428 9111.
www.parks-sa.co.za

Kgalagadi Transfrontier National Park

This vast expanse of Kalahari Desert supports a surprising amount of wildlife, including lions, gemsbok, springbok, wildebeest, eland and many smaller animals. It is one of the best places in South Africa to see cheetah.

Although classified as a desert, much of the Kalahari consists of open, grass-covered plains interspersed with thorn trees and lightly vegetated sand dunes. The former Kalahari Gemsbok National Park (SA) and the Gemsbok National Park (Botswana) have been amalgamated into the Kgalagadi Transfrontier Park which is some 38,000sq km in size.

The park is 260km north of Upington, and distances in the park are large, so careful thought is required when planning a visit.
Many companies also offer tours to the park.

SA National Parks Central Reservations
Tel: (012) 428 9111.
www.parks-sa.co.za

Namaqualand

A vast area of the Northern Cape's huge semi-desert is a Cinderella environment.

Copyright: South African Tourism

The flowers of Namaqualand bloom in early spring

Most of the year, it is harsh and dry, but after the winter rainfall (mid-August to mid-September) it is transformed by millions of brightly coloured daisies, mesembryanthemums, aloes and other flowers. The towns of Springbok, Garies and Hondeklipbaai (Hondeklip Bay) are

---

TRANSFRONTIER PARKS

Several transfrontier parks have been created between South Africa and its neighbours. Many of the more remote regions have declared wildlife areas on both sides of the international border. Authorities have agreed that, where possible, fences should be taken down to allow the free flow of wildlife, and tourists, across the borders. This helps create larger and more diverse wildlife areas under the joint management of the nations involved.

These include the Kgalagadi Transfrontier Park (South Africa and Botswana) and the Great Limpopo Transfrontier Park (South Africa, Zimbabwe and Mozambique). Several other transfrontier parks are being developed.

The dramatic Swartberg Pass

usually the best starting points from which to see the flowers, but it is worth checking with authorities first to find out where rain has fallen.

Springbok is also a good point from which to visit the remote Richtersveld National Park, which is botanically unusual with many rare species. The mountain desert scenery is arid, rocky and cut by jagged ravines. It is home to the semi-nomadic Nama people who have recently won back the right to graze their animals and run some tourist concessions in the park.

De Beers run tours and 4X4 trips to their rich diamond-mining concessions. These concessions are found along restricted areas of the remote windswept western coastline, which has a large population of Cape fur seals.

De Beers Diamond Coast Tours

Kleinsee. Tel: (027) 807 2999.
www. coastaldiamonds.co.za

Central Karoo

The Karoo, in its various forms, extends from the Western Cape deep into the Northern Cape, Free State and Eastern Cape.

Approximately 150–300 million years ago, various deposits were laid down in the vast swamps and soggy jungles that covered the area. Today the region is rich in fossils, both of animals and plants.

Although it is an arid zone, the Karoo supports a wide range of wildlife and farming activity.

The clear and, in winter, cold skies of the Karoo make it a great place for serious astronomers and casual star watchers alike, and South Africa's largest telescope is located at Sutherland.

Karoo National Park

High mountains and wide-open plains are part of the attraction of this 32,000-hectare (76,800-acre) park, which protects a wide range of animals and birdlife. Hundreds of years ago, tens of thousands of springbok migrated across these plains but, these days, numbers are far smaller, due to the guns of countless hunters.

The park preserves a good cross section of typical Karoo habitat and supports springbok, kudu, buffalo and smaller game. No fewer than 20 pairs of black eagles nest in the park.

An award-winning rest camp with Cape-Dutch style cottages and restaurant has been developed.

The nearby town of Beaufort West is the largest in the region and the centre of a large sheep farming community.

South African National Parks Central Bookings
Tel: (012) 428 9111.
www.parks-sa.co.za

Matjiesfontein

This 19th century resort is popular with

Wind pump at sunset

Karoo farmhouse

weekenders from Cape Town. The restored Victorian Lord Milner Hotel and some other buildings in the tiny village are national monuments. The hotel was used as a hospital during the South African War. The luxury Blue Train stops here on its trip between Cape Town and Johannesburg. The town is 260km (162 miles from Cape Town).

Prince Albert and the Swartberg Pass

Sheltering at the foot of the Swartberg Pass is the pretty village of Price Albert, which is a welcome change from the dusty plains of the Karoo.

The steep pass climbs through the Swartberg mountains, and the view across the range and the plains below are spectacular.

Prince Albert farmers take advantage of the good water run-off from the mountains to grow grapes and olives, and the town has several good restaurants. There are lovely walks and hikes in the mountains and around the village, and the rural atmosphere makes a good breakaway destination.

Prince Albert Tourism Bureau
Tel: (023) 541 1366.
www.patourism.co.za

Diamonds

Copyright: South African Tourism

The discovery of diamonds marked a turning point in southern Africa's development from a rural, forgotten corner, dominated by the British Empire, to a repository of riches that in time would touch the lives of nearly everyone in the region. Diamonds are still a source of South Africa's wealth.

The first diamond discovered was the Eureka (1867), near Hopetown in the Northern Cape. Further finds occurred in 1869 on the farms Bultfontein and Dorstfontein. In 1871, fabulously rich finds were made at Colesberg Kopje, which eventually led to the development of Kimberley.

Life was probably hell for the fortune-seekers who had flocked to the site, although some of them did indeed make fortunes – and not just as prospectors.

Entrepreneurs started coaching companies, or provided such necessities as bars. The biggest headache of all was establishing ownership of this diamond-rich territory. It was called Griqualand West by the respective governments of the Free State and the South African Republic, and by the Cape Colony. It had been claimed by the Griqua, who

Copyright: South African Tourism

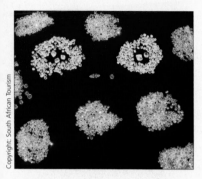

had lived there for 70 years. In the end the British simply annexed it to the Cape (1880).

Kimberley was the cradle of the hugely profitable diamond industry that grew up in southern Africa. No-one could ever have dreamt of the riches that the Big Hole would yield. As digging continued, and the hole got deeper, squabbles broke out as miners struggled to get to their claims at ever more perilous depths.

This led to the amalgamation of smaller workings, heralding the era of the big mining companies. About 20 years after the first diamond had been discovered, the De Beers mine, controlled by Cecil John Rhodes, owned virtually the entire diamond industry. Since Rhodes, and under the Oppenheimer dynasty of Ernest, Harry and now Nicky, it has become one of the world's largest and most profitable mining companies.

Opposite top: Cut and uncut diamonds
Opposite bottom: Diamond-bearing kimberlite and gemstones
Above: Piles of sorted diamonds
Below: Diamond boats, used to collect alluvial diamonds

Western Cape

Variety is the keyword of the Western Cape. Cape Town, sheltered by the famous Table Mountain, is the gateway to this province of mountains, beaches, vineyards and a broad assortment of cultures and traditions. Both the Indian and Atlantic Oceans fringe the Cape coastline. Ranges of high, craggy fold-mountains roll across the province, and in the east thick indigenous forests provide a contrast to the semi-deserts of the Karoo, which forms the northern boundary of the province.

The Western Cape's physical diversity encourages a wide variety of outdoor activity including hiking, mountain-bike riding, kloofing, paragliding, diving, surfing, fishing or good old sunbathing and swimming.

Although lacking the variety of big game that occurs elsewhere in South Africa, the Western Cape boasts a vast diversity of mammal, bird and reptile species with some unique attractions. The *fynbos* vegetation, which dominates

V & A Waterfront, with Table Mountain in the background

The bright old Cape Malay houses of the Bo Kaap

the region, is the richest floral kingdom in the world hosting more than 7,300 species, 65 per cent of which occur nowhere else on the planet. The coast also offers some of the world's best sightings of southern right whales and their newborn calves.

Closer to Cape Town, the many vineyards tempt tourists and locals alike with excellent wine and food. Throughout the region, restaurants reflect the cultural diversity of the population. Along the Cape Peninsula, small towns, including Simon's Town and Kalk Bay, have a seaside atmosphere with many good restaurants, antique shops and interesting history. Cape Town and many of the smaller centres like Darling and Hout Bay have thriving artistic communities. Theatre, music and dance performances offer a constant selection of entertainment and cultural education.

CAPE TOWN

Cape Town is a city of beaches, mountains, good food and wine, diverse culture and a laid-back view of the world. It is also a city of great contrasts, with many poor people living in sub-standard housing, as anyone driving to the airport past the thousands of shacks on the Cape Flats cannot fail to be reminded of. Whatever their economic circumstances, Capetonians pride themselves on knowing how to have fun and how to enjoy the scenic splendour that surrounds them. On weekends, the beaches and mountains attract families out for picnics and the more energetic out riding bikes, hiking, surfing and jogging.

Cape Town Castle

Restaurants, ranging from the formal to the hip and trendy, cluster around the major beaches, the Waterfront, vineyards, and in the City Bowl itself, particularly in Kloof Street and Long Street. Cape Town is the oldest city in the country and some buildings, many of which have been restored, date back to the 17th century. Mosques, synagogues and churches attest to the many cultures that mix in the city, as do the variety of artistic styles and culinary preferences. Although many Capetonians seem to base their lives around the beaches, mountains and restaurants, the city is also home to the Houses of Parliament and several multinational corporations.

Bo Kaap Museum

This museum is in a colourful, predominantly Muslim part of Cape Town and recreates a typical 19th century Malay home. Many of the people who live in the area are descendents of slaves. Nearby is the Auwal Mosque, one of nine in the area.

The Auwal Mosque, in Dorp Street, was built in 1798. It is recommended that visitors use one of the various companies that offer tours through this vibrant neighbourhood.

Bo Kaap Museum
71 Wale Street. Tel: (021) 481 3939.
Open: Mon–Sat 9.30–4pm.
Admission charge.

Cape Flats' Townships

Gugulethu, Khayalitsha, Crossroads and Nyanga are home to the majority of Capetonians, and no visit to the region is complete without visiting these townships. Tour guides take in all the more politically significant areas and will happily stop at local restaurants or roadside cafés. All the townships are within sight of Table Mountain and make a startling contrast to the wealth concentrated on its slopes.

Many township tours also take in the Bo Kaap area and the District Six Museum.

Cape Town Tourism
Tel: (021) 426 4260 or 405 4500.

Castle of Good Hope

Although the Castle was built as a fort in 1666–9, it has never seen battle, and the most exiting skirmishes it has overseen are those caused by the busy Cape Town traffic.

The outstanding William Fehr Collection of paintings, furniture and other items dating back to the arrival of the first White settlers is kept at the Castle, and there is also a military museum. Tours are conducted daily (call for times), and include a visit to the dark and damp dungeon under the main castle. There are two restaurants in the castle grounds.

Buitenkant St. Tel: (021) 787 1249.
Open: daily 9am–4pm.
Admission charge.

Clifton Beach and Camps Bay

These are two of South Africa's trendiest and most image-conscious areas – fashion and money really matter here. The beaches are gleaming stretches of white sand that look like movie sets, although the water is cold. There are no shops near Clifton beach, but vendors sell refreshments.

By day, people visit the beaches to be seen, and in the evenings the bars and restaurants of Camps Bay are packed with well-off people having fun. In summer, it is light until quite late in Cape Town (about 9pm), and Camps Bay is a good place to watch the sun set.

Company's Gardens

The paths through these gardens meander past some of Cape Town's best-known buildings, including the Houses of Parliament, St George's Cathedral, the South African National Gallery and the South African Museum. Many people merely use the gardens as a way of escaping some of the bustle of the city, and on sunny days dozens of office-workers and others sit on the lawns under the large old trees.

The Dutch East India Company established the gardens in 1652 to grow vegetables to supply their staff and passing ships. The gardens are open all day, but be cautious of 'street kids' who sometimes snatch bags or jewellery *(see Box on p128).*
Upper Adderley St.

Cultural History Museum

Part of South Africa's darker history is

Camps Bay

that of slavery in the Cape. This building was first used to house slaves brought to the Cape, and in later years was used as a brothel, a post office, a jail, a library and later housed the Supreme Court. Now a museum, there are displays detailing Cape Town's history and, surprisingly, even material from ancient Greece and the Far East.
49 Adderley St.
Tel: (021) 461 8280.
Open: daily 9.30am–4.30pm.
Admission charge.

Company's Gardens

District Six Museum

A good example of apartheid's brutal policy of racial segregation is presented in the pictures, maps, newspaper articles and displays in this museum. District Six was a thriving community of mixed-race South Africans, until the government of the day decided they should be moved out of sight of central Cape Town and bulldozed the entire neighbourhood.

Some of the workers at the museum used to live in the area, and each has a sad story to tell of how their homes were destroyed. People are slowly moving back into District Six, and tours can be arranged.
25A Buitekant St.
Tel: (021) 461 8745.
www.districtsix.co.za
Open: Mon–Sat 9am–4pm. Closed: Sun.

Gold of Africa Museum

This museum contains a large and unusual collection of gold masks, animals, and other artwork from all over Africa, but primarily West Africa. Goldsmiths from Ghana and Mali are particularly skilled and many examples of their work are on display.

Artefacts from Zimbabwe and elsewhere are also featured in the museum. The building which houses the museum was built in 1783.
Martin Melk House, 96 Strand St.
Tel: (021) 405 1540.
www.goldofafrica.co.za
Open: Mon–Sat 9.30am–5pm.
Closed: Sun.
Admission charge.

Greenmarket Square

This is a good place for some casual shopping while strolling through the centre of the city. At the fleamarket, based in the cobbled square, stallholders sell a huge variety of curios, clothing and odds and ends. There are lots more formal shops in the area and restaurants.
Corner Burg St and Longmarket St.

Groot Constantia

This is one of Cape Town's most elegant buildings, and is the oldest wine estate in the country. Established by Cape Governor, Simon van der Stel, in 1685, the estate has a reputation for fine red wines, but the white wines are pretty good too. Napoleon Bonaparte's time in exile was made a little easier by supplies of wine from this estate!

The Manor House Cultural Museum is well worth a visit too. There are two restaurants and, on good days, you can order a picnic and sit in the tranquil gardens to admire the wonderful views.
Groot Constantia Rd.
Tel: (021) 794 5128.
www.grootconstantia.co.za
Open: daily 10am–5pm.
Admission charge to museum.

Houses of Parliament
During debates, parliament can be pretty noisy with vigorous heckling, but you never know when you may spot a tired MP snoozing! Tour guides help explain the workings of the South African political system and explain the history of the buildings, which were built in 1884 and opened in 1885.
Parliament St.
Tel: (021) 403 3683.
www.parliament.gov.za
Open: Mon–Fri. Tours on the hour from 9am–12pm. Booking required.
Free admission.

Hout Bay fishing harbour

Hout Bay

Although many regard Hout Bay as being a separate town from Cape Town, it is part of the greater city. The Chapman's Peak Drive offers phenomenal views across Hout Bay. Further along, as the road winds along the mountainside, there are also great views of the wide expanse of Noordhoek Beach. There are a variety of hotels and bars, including those on the Mariner's Wharf, which are good places for sundowners.

A toll is charged for vehicles using Chapman's Peak Drive.

Irma Stern Museum

Some of Irma Stern's best expressionist works are displayed here, as well as her personal collection of international art. Stern (1904–96) lived in the house for nearly 40 years, and her studio has been kept as it was when she worked there. The museum sometimes hosts exhibitions of other artists too.

Cecil Rd, Rosebank.
Tel: (021) 685 5686.
www.irmastern.co.za
Open: Tues–Sat 10am–5pm.
Small admission charge.

Iziko-SA National Gallery

Some art-lovers spend a whole morning or longer at this gallery which is considered by many to be one of the best in the country. There are comprehensive displays of South African and international art from different periods including paintings, beadwork, sculptures, ceramics and textiles. Some exhibitions are changed regularly, but others are permanent.

Government Ave, Company's Gardens.
Tel: (021) 456 1628.
www.museums.org.za
Open: Tues–Sun 10am–5pm.
Admission charge, Sun free.

Kirstenbosch National Botanical Garden

A seemingly endless variety of flowers, succulents, trees and shrubs adorn the carefully tended gardens and manicured lawns that sweep up towards the steep, forested mountain slopes above. Kirstenbosch's splendid setting is alone worth the visit, but these gardens, founded in 1913, are famous among

Iziko-SA National Gallery

Kirstenbosch National Botanical Garden

botanists worldwide for the variety of indigenous plants grown here.

There are also many rare plants of scientific and educational interest. Through careful selection, there are displays of flowers throughout the year, and in summer concerts are held in the gardens. A variety of walks ranging from short ambles to a 6km (3,7-mile) trail have been laid out in the 560-hectare (1,344-acre) gardens. A restaurant serves light meals and there is a shop.

Kirstenbosch National Botanical Garden

Tel: (021) 762 1166.
www.kirstenbosch.co.za
Open: Apr–Aug 8am–6pm,
Sept–Mar 8am–7pm.
Admission charge.

Long Street

Antique shops, book stores, music stores and any number of bars and restaurants line this street, which has a rather Bohemian atmosphere. The clubs may be somewhat smoky and noisy and might not be to everyone's taste, but Long Street provides an indispensable view into Cape Town's young multicultural set.

Michaelis Collection

Works by Rembrandt, Frans Hals, Jan van Goyen and other 16th and 17th century Dutch and Flemish artists form the core of this museum. Most were donated by Sir Max Michaelis in 1914, and are displayed in the Old Town House building. This building was

built in 1755, and was once used as the city hall.
Greenmarket Square. Tel: (021) 481 3933.
www.museums.org.za
Open: Mon–Fri 10am–5pm,
Sat 10am–4pm.
Small admission charge.

Pan African Market

More than 30 stallholders sell a variety of African arts from all over the continent. The market is billed as 'Africa under a roof'. People from countries as far away as Mali, Nigeria, Cameroon and Ethiopia sell their work here, and other migrants gather at the Kalukuta Republik Book Café to chat, have a meal or listen to poetry readings.
76 Long St.
Tel: (021) 426 4478.
wwwpanafrican.co.za
Open: daily 9am–6pm.

Robben Island

'The Island', just off Cape Town, holds an almost mythical aura for many South Africans as a place of banishment and

The Quarry on Robben Island where Mandela was forced to work

Trendy Long Street

incarceration. It was here that Nelson Mandela was held for most of his 27 years imprisonment. His cell and those of other leaders are visited by thousands of people, many doing so in a form of pilgrimage to these icons.

The prison has been turned into a museum explaining the role of the leaders of the liberation struggle and the brutal history of the island, which, since the 17th century, was used as a penal colony.

Much of the seashore surrounding the island is a nature reserve, and African penguins are common.
Tel: (021) 419 1300.
www.robben-island.org.za
Tours: Ferries leave the V&A Waterfront hourly 8am–3pm. Book in advance.
Summer sunset tours at 5pm & 6pm.
Admission charge.

South African Museum and Planetarium

South Africa's oldest museum has many exhibitions displaying cultural history, wildlife, rock art and fossils. In the neighbouring planetarium, the southern

skies can be explored. The museum is large and takes a while to explore.

Some of the more unusual displays are the Linton Panel containing San rock art and the Lydenburg Heads, some of the earliest African sculptures. In the Whale Well, there is, among other displays, a complete 20m-long skeleton of a blue whale.

25 Queen Victoria St.
Tel: (021) 481 3800.
www.museums.org.za
Open: 10am–5pm. Closed: Christmas Day & Good Friday.
Admission charge.

Signal Hill and Lions Head

These two landmarks provide fantastic views of central Cape Town, the Waterfront, the beaches at Camps Bay, Clifton and also Robben Island. They also help emphasise the sheer scale of Table Mountain soaring over the city.

Every day, the Noon Gun, an old cannon, is fired from Signal Hill with an explosion that is audible all over Cape Town. The tradition dates back to 1822 when the Noon Gun was used to allow ships in harbour to set their clocks accurately.

Once you have checked your watch, the nearby restaurant is a good place for a bite to eat or a drink.

Military Rd, Signal Hill.
Tel: (021) 787 1257.
Open: Mon–Sat. Free admission.

Table Mountain and Cableway

"The view", wrote botanist William Burchell in 1822 after being inspired to climb Table Mountain "is singularly grand". It remains so now. For just under four centuries the 1,087m (3,532ft) high mountain has been the focal point of Cape Town, influencing

TABLE MOUNTAIN NATIONAL PARK

Nearly every mountain between Table Mountain and Cape Point, a distance of some 60km (37 miles), falls into this park (formerly Cape Peninsula National Park). The park is the richest botanical area for its size on earth, and a variety of mammals, birds and fish are also protected. It is an unusual national park in that it falls entirely within a metropolitan area. There are hundreds of kilometres of hiking trails along the mountains and beaches, although there is limited accommodation within the park and at Cape Point. Most people merely stay in urban areas and walk straight onto beaches or the mountainsides.

Tel: (021) 701 8692.
www.tmnp.co.za

Table Mountain cableway

Thunder City jets

weather patterns and even people's attitudes. It forms a bold northern front of a high range stretching 60km (37 miles) to Cape Point. The mountain's slopes and ravines offer dozens of walks and climbs from the easy to the severe, while the cable car, transports passengers to the summit's viewing platforms and restaurants.
Cable station.
Tel: (021) 424 8181.
www.tablemountain.co.za
Opening hours vary according to season. Also check weather conditions as the cable station may close in bad weather.

Thunder City

Thunder City is one of the few places in the world tourists can go for a flip in a combat jet but, be warned, the flights are for the rich only. Even if you can't afford a sub-sonic flight over the Cape Peninsula, the aircraft and other memorabilia can be viewed at close range when they are not flying. Thunder City has an English Electric Lightning, BAe Buccaneer and Hawker Hunter on display.
Cape Town International Airport.
Tel: (021) 934 8007.
www.thundercity.com
Open: Mon–Sun 9am–5pm.
Admission charge.

Two Oceans Aquarium

Spending time at the Two Oceans is bit like taking a fantastic scuba-diving trip without getting wet. Shoals of deep-sea fish, sharks, rays, coral reef displays,

turtles, seals and penguins all provide hours of education and entertainment. For those who are prepared to get wet, there are interactive displays where children can touch some sea creatures, and qualified divers can even arrange to swim in the tank where the sharks live.

The aquarium is home to fish and marine life from both the South Africa's warm east coast and the cold west coast waters.

Dock Rd, V&A Waterfront.
Tel: (021) 418 3823.
www.aquarium.co.za
Open: daily 9.30am–6pm.
Admission charge.

Two Oceans Aquarium

Victoria and Alfred Waterfront (V&A Waterfront)

Once disused harbour land, the Waterfront is a vast collection of hugely popular shops, curio stores, restaurants, cinemas and museums. Many of the restaurants overlook the harbour, and in good weather the walkways and piers fill up with people enjoying a drink or a meal, while watching activity in the working harbour.

Several hotels are part of the complex. Ferries leave from here for Robben Island and sunset cruises along the coast. *Open: daily.*

The Victoria and Alfred Waterfront

Tour: The Cape Peninsula

The Cape Peninsula's mountain chain curves south from Cape Town, dips at Constantia Nek, rises at Constantiaberg, falls away over Silvermine to the Fish Hoek Valley, then swings past Simon's Town to the southeast. For 12km (7,5 miles), before finally tumbling into the sea at Cape Point, it blends into the unspoiled wilderness of the Cape of Good Hope Nature Reserve (now part of the Table Mountain National Park).

Allow one day. In the centre of Cape Town, take Somerset Road at its junction with Buitengracht Street and continue along Main Road through Sea Point to the M6.

Simon's Town on the Peninsula

1 The Atlantic Seaboard
Sea Point's Promenade is a favourite stretch for slow walks or faster jogs.

Further on, at Bantry Bay, little Saunders Rock Beach with its tidal pool offers safe bathing.

Sea Point

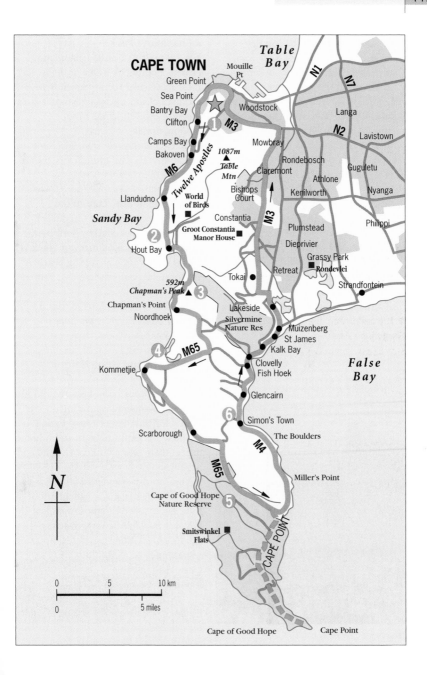

Beyond, Clifton has the country's most fashionable beaches. Next door, Camps Bay's beaches are sprawled dramatically at the foot of the magnificent Twelve Apostles. The road winds on past Bakoven to Llandudno, picturesquely climbing up steep slopes, with Sandy Bay, a nudist beach beyond. *The M6 climbs the hill above Llandudno, then descends towards Hout Bay.*

2 Hout Bay

Wood *(hout)* was obtained here for early Cape Town buildings. The town has a lovely beach, waterfront development and a fishing harbour, which is the centre of the snoek industry and base of the crayfishing fleet. The World of Birds bird sanctuary is in the Hout Bay Valley. *Return to the M6, and follow the signs to Chapman's Peak.*

The dramatic False Bay coast

3 Chapman's Peak

The 10km drive around Chapman's Peak to Noordhoek is one of the world's most spectacular scenic passes, with exceptional views across the bay. It gives access to excellent climbs and mountain walks.
From Noordhoek, follow the M6 from which, after the first traffic lights, the M65 branches right to Kommetjie.

4 Noordhoek and Kommetjie

Noordhoek's lovely 6km (3,7 miles) Long Beach is favoured by horseback riders. At its end, Kommetjie is a quiet village with a popular surfing beach. A shallow tidal pool provides safe bathing for children.
From Kommetjie, the M65 continues through Scarborough to the Cape of Good Hope.

5 Cape of Good Hope Nature Reserve

This magnificent 7,750-hectare (19,150 acre) nature reserve is now included in the Table Mountain National Park. It straddles the Peninsula's tip and is home to mountain zebra, bontebok, eland and baboons.

There are drives and places to picnic and swim. The view from Cape point across False Bay, so called because it was often mistaken for Table Bay, is spectacular.
Tel: (021) 780 9204.
www.cpnp.co.za
Open: daily.
Admission charge.

At the exit, turn right if you want to visit the southern tip, then return north, turning right on to the M4 to Simon's Town.

6 False Bay

The approach to Simon's Town is via The Boulders, where the swimming, among huge boulders, is shared with a colony of African penguins. Simon's Town, South Africa's largest naval base, is a quaint seaside town, beyond which is Fish Hoek – a popular resort with wide, safe beaches.

Kalk Bay, with antique, junk and craft shops, is home to the False Bay fishing fleet. Beyond, St James has a small beach with a tidal pool. Alongside it, Muizenberg's magnificent beach offers safe bathing. Visit the Natale Labia Museum and Rhodes Cottage memorial museum.

Continue on the M4 past Lakeside, and follow the signs to the M3 and the city.

Simon's Town Museum
Court Rd. Tel: (021) 786 3046.
www.simonstown.com
Open: Tues–Fri 10am–4pm, Sat 11am–4pm. Closed: Sun, Christmas Day & Good Friday.
Admission charge.
Natale Labia Museum
192 Main Rd, Muizenberg.
Tel: (021) 788 4106.
www.labia.co.za
Open: Mon–Sat.
Admission charge.
Rhodes Cottage
Main Rd, Muizenberg.
Tel: (021) 788 1816.
Open: 9am–4pm.
Donation.

Hout Bay from Chapman's Peak

The southern Cape is one of the best places in the world for land-based whale watching. Every year, between June and November, large numbers of southern right whales are spotted all along the coastline.

The whales migrate from the cold southern oceans to the warmer coastal waters to give birth and mate, before beginning the long journey south to their primary feeding grounds again. They are often seen close inshore with their calves, which measure about 5m (16,4ft) at birth.

Humpback whales are also often spotted, although in smaller numbers and usually further north along the KwaZulu-Natal coast as they migrate to their calving and mating grounds near Madagascar. Both species of whales tend to gather in small groups.

The largest number of southern right whales usually congregate between False Bay and Hermanus, where the sea cliffs make ideal viewing platforms from which to watch them.

The whales sometimes 'breach', lifting most of their bodies out of the water, before crashing in again with a huge splash. They also 'sail' with their heads underwater and their tail flukes protruding into the air. Humpbacks display more regularly and in even more spectacular fashion. It is believed that these displays are part of courtship and other social rituals.

Both species of whale were hunted heavily in the past. The southern right whale is so called because it floats when killed, and was considered the 'right' whale to hunt, but since hunting restrictions were imposed, their numbers have begun increasing fairly quickly.

The whale-watching industry has boomed in recent years, particularly around Hermanus, and several companies specialise in both land- and boat-based whale watching. The boats are strictly regulated, and it is illegal to approach the whales too closely.

There are a wide variety of B&Bs and hotels in the area, as well as good restaurants. The area is busy in whale-watching season, which usually reaches

Copyright: South African Tourism

its peak in September and October.

Many other species of whale occur in South African waters, as do twelve species of dolphin. Common, bottlenose, dusky and humpbacked dolphins are often seen along the coast. Near Sodwana Bay on the KwaZulu-Natal coast, swimmers often mingle with dolphins near shallow reefs.

Southern Right Whales

The southern right whale grows to a maximum length of 15–17m (49–55ft) and weighs 50,000–65,000kg (50–65 tons). They are not deep divers and seldom stay submerged for than 20 minutes. They eat small crustaceans (krill) found relatively close to the surface. Little is known of their social structure, but the mothers form very strong bonds with their calves.

Humpback Whales

These whales grow to about 14m (44ft) in length and feed on small crustaceans (krill) and small fish. They weigh between 25,000–40,000kg (25–40 tons).

Humpback whales are well known for their 'songs' a series of squeaks, moans and whistles of varying pitch, which can last up to 30 minutes. They usually stay submerged for a fairly short time, seldom longer than 15 minutes.

Opposite: Whale watching
Above: Hermanus

Winemaking

The South African wine industry has grown by leaps and bounds in recent years and has developed a considerable export market. There are hundreds of small boutique vineyards scattered throughout the Western Cape, cheekily rubbing shoulders with the big well-established vineyards.

Franschhoek, Stellenbosch and Paarl are the best-known South African wine-producing regions, but clever winemakers in towns like Worcester, Robertson and Montagu, some 180km (110 miles) from Cape Town, have now leapt into the market. Wealthy business people and foreigners who vie with each other to hire the best and most innovative winemakers have bought numerous vineyards.

Winemaking and fruit-growing provide economic sustenance for entire valleys in the Western Cape. Even people not directly involved in the cellars earn their livelihoods from associated businesses like restaurants, craft shops, cheese-making and tourism.

Many vineyards offer wine-tasting tours and others run good restaurants on their properties too. Each region – all in all there are 17 recognised wine routes – offers organised tours, although many tourists opt to drive themselves and spend a few days in the

scenic winelands.

Whitewashed, gabled houses, surrounded by vines sheltering in valleys beneath high fold-mountains, make for picturesque touring conditions ideal for enjoying good wine and food.

All the regions offer other activities, including horse riding and hiking, and trout, yellowfish and bass fishing. There are a wide range of B&Bs, guest farms and lodges throughout the winelands.

Although experts consider South African red wines to be superior to the whites, many new winemaking techniques and cultivars have been developed to make the most of local conditions. Cabernet Sauvignon, Shiraz and Merlot are the most common reds, although the local Pinotage cultivars are also popular. There is a large range of whites with Chardonnay, Chenin Blanc and Sauvignon Blanc being the choice of many cellars.

South Africa's winemaking history dates back some 350 years, and the first vineyards were planted in 1655. South Africa also makes excellent sherry and fortified wines (better known as Port, although European Union trade regulations forbid the use of the more familiar name).

Some vineyards can trace their origins back to the arrival of the French Huguenots in the 17th century. Brandy is also produced in some areas, and there is even a brandy-tasting route.

It is well worth buying one of the many wine guides on offer. One of the best is John Platter's *Guide to the Wines of South Africa*.

Opposite top: Groot Constantia Wine Estate
Opposite below: Grapevines
Below: Vineyards near Darling

Elsewhere in the Western Cape

There are dozens of beautiful places within easy reach of Cape Town. The best known are the winelands which stretch inland from the city boundaries through Stellenbosch, Franshhoek and Paarl and then along the east coast to Walker Bay. There are good beaches all along the coast between Cape Town and the Garden Route and mountain ranges cut through the entire region. Many pretty villages and towns are also within easy reach of Cape Town.

Paarl vineyards

Franschhoek

The beautiful Franschhoek Valley is one of South Africa's premier wine-producing areas, and has become an extremely fashionable place to live and to holiday.

In 1688, the Cape Governor, Simon van der Stel, granted French Huguenot

Franschhoek vineyard

refugees land in the valley which earned the area its name meaning 'French Corner'.

Today most estates in the valley offer wine-tasting, and many have excellent restaurants. The region caters specifically for tourists, and there are many art and curio shops as well as delicatessens offering local products. There are many scenic drives through the valley, and it is also worth visiting the Huguenot Museum.

Franschhoek Vale'e Tourisme
Tel: (021) 876 3606.
www. franschhoek.org.za

Stellenbosch

Stellenbosch is perhaps the town most often associated with South African wine, and was founded by Dutch Governor Simon van der Stel in 1679. The town, its culture and its economy revolve around the wine industry and the University of Stellenbosch.

There are many fine examples of Cape Dutch architecture, with some of the best examples in Dorp, Church and Drotsdy streets. There are a variety of museums for those tired of tasting wine and eating good food in the surrounding vineyards.

Stellenbosch Tourism Bureau
Tel: (021) 883 3584.
www.istellenbosch.org.za

Paarl

Paarl (The Pearl) is another important wine-growing centre and, although it

Stellenbosch

Langebaan is a popular weekend spot with a good beach and relaxed restaurants

does not share the charm of Stellenbosch or Franschhoek, the wines are no less delicious.

Although the town was established in the early 18th century, the area had been settled and farmed since the late 1600s.

Despite the town focusing on wine farming, other agriculture is also important. There are pleasant walks in the nearby Paarl Mountain Nature Reserve.

Paarl Tourism Bureau
Tel: (021) 872 3829.
www.paarlonline.com

Langebaan

The Langebaan Lagoon forms part of the West Coast National Park, and is an internationally important birding wetland. Whales are sometimes spotted from the shore, and in August and September there are usually good

STREET KIDS

'Street kids' are homeless youngsters who live on the streets of South Africa's larger cities. Many abuse drugs, and in particular sniff glue. Sadly, some of these children resort to crime as a means of surviving. They usually work in groups with one child distracting the victim as the others snatch bags, necklaces or any other item they can grab. Many also beg at traffic lights.

It is best to resist giving them money, because it is often used to buy glue. There are several organisations and shelters that try to offer these children better lives.

Kite surfing in Langebaan

showings of wild flowers. The nearby village of Langebaan is a useful stopover when visiting the Park, which is some 100km (60 miles) north of Cape Town.

46km north of Langebaan is the small fishing village of Paternoster, which is well known for its crayfish and other seafood. Many people stopover for weekend lunches and to photograph the whitewashed fishermen's villages.

The nearby Columbine Nature Reserve protects a variety of coastal plants and wetland birds.

Langebaan Tourism Bureau
Tel: (022) 772 1515.
www.langebaaninfo.com

Ceres

This town can only be reached by one of three scenic mountain passes, and is one of South Africa's premier deciduous-fruit growing areas.

Stall near Ceres

Oudtshoorn humour – ostriches don't fly and you can't make cheese from them

Ceres is named after the Roman goddess of fruitfulness, and has a good climate with more than 230 days of sunshine a year on average.

Various tours of fruit farms can be undertaken, as well as visits to nearby game reserves, San rock art sites, hikes, mountain biking and fishing. The town is about an hour and forty minutes drive from Cape Town.

Ceres Tourism
Tel: (023) 316 1287.
www.ceres.org.za

Cederberg Wilderness Area

The 162,000-hectare (400,302-acre) wilderness area covers the rugged peaks and valleys, which provide good hiking and a huge variety of plant life. The towns of Citrusdal and Clanwilliam make good bases from which to explore the mountains and surrounding farms. After good rains, many flowers cover the *veld*, although they are not usually as prolific as those further north in Namaqualand *(see Northern Cape section*

on pp98–103).
The area is about 220km (137 miles) north of Cape Town.

Cape Nature Conservation
Tel: (021) 426 0723 for hiking permits.
www.capenature.org.za
Citrusdal Tourism Bureau
Tel: (022) 921 3210.
www.citrusdal.com
Clanwilliam Tourism Bureau
Tel: (027) 482 2361.
www.clanwilliam.info

Tulbagh

Church Street in Tulbagh has no fewer than 32 national monuments – all classical Cape Dutch buildings, with whitewashed walls and thatched roofs, dating back as far as 1754. Most of the cottages were severely damaged or destroyed in a rare earthquake in 1969, but were all lovingly restored to their former glory.

Ostrich eggs in Oudtshoorn

Tulbach is packed with pretty Cape Dutch houses

The Oude Kerk Volksmuseum contains displays telling the story of the earthquake and the restoration project. The De Oude Drostdy Museum, which was built in 1804, is a fine example of Cape Dutch architecture.

The area also has many wine estates, restaurants and B&Bs. The more energetic can take horseback or bicycle rides through the pretty valley, or undertake hikes of varying strenuousness.

Tulbagh Tourism Bureau
Tel: (023) 230 1348.
www.tulbaghtourism.co.za

Swartberg Pass

Cape Agulhas/Arniston
Cape Agulhas is Africa's most southerly tip, despite the commonly held belief that it is Cape Point. Nearby, the thatched-roofed and white-walled houses of Arniston have been declared national monuments, and white, windswept beaches have a harsh beauty.

Cape Agulhas is about 100km (60 miles) south of Swellendam. On the way, the Shipwreck Museum at Bredasdorp has a display of artefacts collected from the many ships wrecked along this coast.

The nearby De Hoop Nature Reserve offers protection to a wide array of vegetation, mammals and sealife. The marine reserve along the shoreline extends 5km (3 miles) out to sea. Whales are often spotted here, usually from August to October.

Witsand Tourism
Tel: (028) 537 1011.
www.witsand.com

CAPE MOUNTAIN PASSES

Dozens of steep mountain passes with magnificent scenery are a feature of the Western Cape and the Garden Route. A whole range of skilfully designed roads cut from the coast through the fold-mountains to the interior. Further inland, the passes are no less spectacular, and many are worth travelling through merely for the scenery. Some of the better known are the Swartberg Pass near Prince Albert, the Du Toits Kloof Pass (use the old main road) between Paarl and Worcester, the Prince Alfred Pass near Knysna, the Franschhoek Pass and the Outeniqua Pass near George.

Oudtshoorn and the Cango Caves

Oudtshoorn used to be the ostrich feather capital of the world, and exported tons of these once-popular fashion items to Europe in the late 19th and early 20th centuries. Even now, ostriches are widely farmed, but these days meat and leather are more important products than feathers, although many farms put on ostrich shows and races. Tourists can also ride on the ungainly creatures, the largest of the world's birds.

Many Victorian and older buildings line the streets of the town. The chambers and stalactites and stalagmites of the Cango Caves lure tourists underground some 32km (20 miles) north of Oudtshoorn. An hour-long guided tour takes visitors through the large main caves, but the system runs much deeper under the Swartberg mountains.

Oudtshoorn Tourism Bureau
Tel: (044) 272 8226.
Cango Caves
Tel: (044) 272 7410. Open: daily.
Admission charge and guided tours.

Drostdy Museum, Swellendam

Swellendam

South Africa's third-oldest town is built on the slopes of the Langeberg mountains and close to the wide Breede River – scenery that complements the whitewashed walls of the town's many old buildings.

The town was established in 1743 and soon after, in 1746, the building which now houses the Drostdy Museum, was constructed. The museum incorporates several other nearby buildings with displays of period furniture, clothing and art. The Dutch Reformed Church, although only built in 1911, includes Baroque, Gothic and eastern architecture.

The nearby Marloth Nature Reserve has a network of hiking trails through the mountains.

Swellendam Tourism Bureau
Tel: (028) 514 2675.
Drostdy Museum
Tel: (028) 514 1138. Open: daily.

Bontebok National Park

The beautiful bontebok antelope has prospered in this national park, which is South Africa's smallest. The antelope was hunted to the verge of extinction, and this park has played an important role in the recovery of the bontebok, which only occurs in the Western Cape. Cape mountain zebras and a variety of smaller antelope, birds and reptiles also occur here. The reserve protects an important area of shrub *fynbos*, which has been ploughed up for wheat fields elsewhere in the region.

The park is close to Swellendam.
Bookings: **SA National Parks Central Reservations.** *Tel: (012) 428 9111.*
www.parks-sa.co.za

Tour: The Garden Route

The Garden Route is one of South Africa's most scenic drives. Skirting the Indian Ocean, and occasionally dipping inland through lush nature reserves, forest, high mountain passes and lakes, this is a coast of holiday-towns and resorts. The Knysna and Tsitsikamma regions are covered in dense indigenous forest, and in places steep cliffs drop directly into the sea. Accommodation is plentiful, and activities range from hiking and walking to water sports and golf. The region is very busy at Christmas and Easter.

Allow at least three days. Start in George.

Garden Route, Storms River Bridge

1 George and the Wilderness National Park

The high, forested Outeniqua Mountains form the backdrop to George – one of the biggest towns along the Garden Route. The internationally renowned Erinvale Golf Course is on the outskirts of town and an important stop for any golfer. The town, which was founded in 1811, has various museums and buildings of interest including the Outeniqua Railway Museum.

The Outeniqua Choo-Tjoe steam train runs to George, stopping at Knysna along a spectacular route *(see train rides pp46–7)*.

The Wilderness National Park just east of George protects a series of coastal lakes that form an important refuge for water birds.

Outeniqua Railway Museum and Outeniqua Choo-Tjoe
Tel: (044) 801 8288.
Museum open: Mon–Sat 8am–5pm.
The train runs Mon–Sat, but call to confirm times as the schedule sometimes changes.

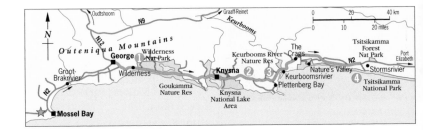

Knysna Heads

Tsitsikamma National Park

Continue along the N2 for 62km to Knysna.

2 Knysna and the Swartberg Pass

Built around the huge, scenic Knysna Lagoon, this town has grown into one of South Africa's most popular tourist resorts.

Open to the sea between high sandstone cliffs called The Heads, the lagoon is an important nursery for fish and other sealife, and is also used for a wide variety of watersports. There are many good beaches near Knysna including Knoetze (10km/6 miles north), which has a luxurious lodge built in the form of a castle and broad secluded beaches surrounded by forest.

Nearby, the exceptionally scenic Swartberg Pass climbs through South Africa's largest patch of indigenous high forest – some 36,000 hectares (88,956 acres) containing yellowwood and stinkwood trees.

Continue along the N2 to Plettenberg Bay.

3 Plettenberg Bay and Robberg Peninsula

'Plett' is one of South Africa's most fashionable beach resorts. The long, broad, gently curved beach attracts many sun-worshippers at Christmas, but out of season it is quiet. The Robberg

Plettenberg Bay

Peninsula, which is part of the Robberg Nature and Marine Reserve juts out into the sea south of the town and offers pleasant walks and broad vistas. Nearby, Keurbooms River also has good beaches and a river estuary, which many people use for canoeing.

Continue along the N2 to the Tsitsikamma National Park.

4 Tstitsikamma National Park

Running for about 80km (50 miles) along the coast, and 5km (3 miles) out to sea, the park is a spectacular ribbon of forest deeply incised by rivers that have cut their way through the mountains to the sea. The indigenous forest still has some examples of huge yellowwood trees, and a variety of hikes and walks meander through the forest.

The 5-day Otter Trail hike takes in the area in all its splendour, as the path follows the coast along high cliffs and through the forest and river crossings.

Otter Trail bookings can be made through South African National Parks Central Reservations, and need to be made as long as a year in advance. *Tel: (012) 248 9111.* *www.parks-sa.co.za*

Knysna Waterfront

Lesotho and Swaziland

Although these tiny nations are both independent, their tourism industries are closely linked to South Africa. Most tourists visiting these countries will usually have travelled to South Africa first. Both countries are poor and predominantly rural. Swaziland has a pleasant climate, although parts can be hot in summer and Lesotho is very mountainous and cold in winter. Swaziland has several good hiking trails and game reserves. The highlands of Lesotho are well suited to pony trekking.

Lesotho

The high Maluti and Drakensberg mountains dominate most of this tiny Kingdom's scenery. Life among the rugged mountains is harsh, and heavy snowfalls with temperatures way below freezing are common in winter. Many of

A Basotho man with his traditional hat and blanket

the mountain peaks are higher than 2,500m (8,125ft), and no point of the country is lower than 1,000m (3,300ft) above sea level.

Several companies run pony trekking operations and guided hikes. 4X4 trips across the mountains are also available. The horse, or more specifically Basotho pony (a small, stocky, shaggy-coated horse), is the primary source of transport for many people in the mountains. Although crops are grown at lower levels, most people living at high altitude depend on sheep, goats and, to a lesser degree, cattle herding for a living.

Lesotho is entirely surrounded by South Africa, and most of its citizens earn their livelihoods there. The capital city of Maseru has some interesting craft stores, but the real beauty of the country lies in the mountains, waterfalls and deep valleys.

Swaziland

This small, predominantly rural kingdom is sandwiched between South Africa's eastern border and

Mozambique. Many Swazis have relatives living in South Africa on whom they are economically dependent. Even so, Swaziland has a distinct cultural identity that sets it apart from its much larger neighbour.

The Milwane Game Reserve, set in the fertile Ezulweni Valley, offers good game viewing and horse riding. Further north, the hills of Malalotja Nature Reserve are an excellent hiking destination. The Ezulweni valley has several hotels, golf courses and craft and art shops.

The capital Mbabane is 360km (224 miles) from Johannesburg by road. The border is open from 6am–9pm. Some nationalities require visas.

Swazi crafts on sale near Mbabane

Swazi women in traditional dress

Shopping

South Africa has a huge variety of goods to tempt both the casual souvenir-hunters and serious shoppers. Prices vary: shopping malls and high streets, particularly those in tourist areas, tend to be the most expensive, market stalls less so and roadside vendors the cheapest. But, just as the prices vary, so does quality, and shoppers should be cautious when buying at the roadside. Market and roadside vendors expect to bargain, but shop owners in upmarket malls are less flexible and seldom oblige with lower prices.

The Paddagang wine store

WHERE TO SHOP
Antiques
Antiques have risen in price in recent years, but many dealers sell quality products that may tempt knowledgeable buyers.

For a list of the shops, phone the **South African Antique Dealers' Association** *Tel: (011) 880 2387.*
www.saada.co.za

West African masks for sale at the Rosebank African Market

Curios and Carvings

A wide range of wooden masks, carved animals, wooden headrests, beadwork and weaving from all over Africa are sold at markets and by roadside vendors. The quality of some of these products is extremely good, and knowledgeable buyers should be able to make reasonable buys.

Many of these products are sold by migrants from elsewhere in Africa, and chatting with them about their travels can be an interesting experience. Some people take weeks to get to South Africa, travelling by bus or truck with their goods.

Be cautious when buying pottery, carvings and other wooden products at the roadside or at markets. Examine the carvings for cracks that are sometimes disguised with wood filler or shoe polish. Try to establish whether pottery or ceramic items have been properly fired, especially when shopping in rural areas.

Gemstones and Jewellery

Many South African dealers sell top-quality gems and jewellery, and tourists benefit from a VAT (14 per cent) rebate on leaving the country. The jeweller with assist you with the paperwork. This rebate only applies in shops accredited to the Jewellery Council of South Africa. **Jewellery Council of South Africa** *Tel: (011) 807 4681.*

Wild Animal Products

Various wild animal products, including trophies, skins, leather belts and shoes are sold at markets and in shops. Whatever one's view on buying these products, it should be remembered that many countries have strict rules concerning the importation of animal products. It is also illegal to sell ivory and some other animal products, including the skin of the African rock python.

Should you be offered ivory or any other animal product you suspect to be illegal, it is best to notify the police or conservation authorities. Youngsters at the side of the road commonly sell tortoises, but this trade is illegal and should be reported.

Wine

Nearly all cellars are willing to ship wine overseas. Local wines are usually a good buy in comparison with international prices. Wine dealers will also be able to advise on customs limitations on quantities that may be imported to various countries.

Part of the Spier Wine Cellar range

Addy Hoyle Gallery, Clarens

BOOKS AND MAPS
Exclusive Books and **CNA** stores have branches throughout the country.
See telephone directory.

Cape Town
Clarke's Bookshop
Rare and second-hand books, prints and maps, books on South Africa.
277 Long St, 8001.
Tel: (021) 423 5739.
www.clarkesbooks.co.za

Durban
Adams & Co
341 West St. Tel: (031) 304 8571.

Johannesburg
Collectable Books
Antiquarian books, maps, prints and Africana. Also small oils and watercolours.
No 6 The Village, 80 Tyrone Ave, Parkview.
Tel: (011) 636 8320.

CURIOS, ARTS AND CRAFTS
Cape Town
Heartworks
South African ceramics, beadwork and other items for the home.
98 Kloof St. Tel: (021) 424 8419.

Clarens
Addy Hoyle
Art gallery, mainly local paintings of landscapes, fantasy birds, animals and other works.
Clarens, Free State. Tel: (058) 256 1832.
www.addyhoyle.co.za

Durban
Africa Art Gallery
Painting, sculptures and other works by some of South Africa's best artists.
Granada Centre, Umhlanga Rocks.
Tel: (031) 561 2661.
www.africaartgallery.co.za

Johannesburg
Kim Sacks Gallery and School of Ceramics
Selection of art, jewellery and ceramics.
153 Jan Smuts Ave, Parkwood.
Tel: (011) 447 5804.

Art Africa
Ethnic arts and collectables from many parts of sub-Saharan Africa.
62 Tyrone Ave, Parkview.
Tel: (011) 486 2052.

Selling carpets, Kingdom Weavers, KwaZulu-Natal

KwaZulu-Natal Midlands
Kingdom Weavers
African rugs, tapestries and other items.
Curry's Post, Balgowan.
Tel: (033) 234 3144.
www. kingdomweavers.co.za

JEWELLERY AND GEMSTONES
Cape Town
Olga Jewellery Design Studio
Skilfully designed jewellery of all types which can be made to personal preferences.
Victoria Wharf. Tel: (021) 419 8016.

Johannesburg
Charles Grieg
100-year-old family business at the forefront of South African jewellery.
Shop U25, Sandton City.
Tel: (011) 783 3174.

MARKETS
Many cities, towns and villages hold markets on weekends. Check with local tourist authorities for locations and times.

Cape Town
Green Point Fleamarket
Everything and anything from art and clothes to cheese and biltong.
Green Point Stadium. Open: Sun & some public holidays, weather permitting.

Johannesburg
Newtown Market Africa
Cosmopolitan Saturday hub. Antique African costume, masks, junk, beads.
Newtown Cultural Precinct. Open: Sat 9am–4pm.

Durban
Amphitheatre Market
Fleamarket with over 700 stalls.
North Beach. Open: Sun.

OUTDOOR EQUIPMENT
Cape Town
Cape Union Mart
Gear for camping, climbing and
hiking.
Victoria Wharf, The Waterfront.
Tel: toll free 0800 034 000. Branches
nationwide.

Surf Centre
Beach and casual clothing, wetsuits and
the like. Primarily women's wear, but
has men's section.
45 On Castle Building, Castle St.
Tel: (021) 423 7853.

Johannesburg
Outdoor Warehouse
Tents, camping, hiking equipment and
everything for life outdoors.
8 Tungsten St, Strijdom Park,
Randburg.
Tel: (011) 792 8331.
Several branches elsewhere.

Cape Union Mart International
Everything for the outdoors from
pocketknives to sleeping bags.
Hyde Park Shopping Mall.
Tel: (011) 325 5038.
Branches nationwide.

SHOPPING MALLS
Cape Town
Cavendish Square
High-quality shopping, cinemas,
restaurants.

Al fresco dining

Colourful curio shops on the Garden Route

Dreyer St, Claremont.
Tel: (021) 657 5600.
www.cavendish.co.za

Durban
Gateway Theatre of Shopping
Shopping, leisure and entertainment
under one roof. Also extreme sports
facilities.
Durban North. Tel: (031) 566 2332.
www.gatewayworld.co.za

Johannesburg
Rosebank Mall
Fashionable shopping, cinemas,
restaurants and fleamarkets on Sundays.
The Zone opposite the Mall is a trendy
hangout for teenagers.

Pretoria
Menlyn Park Shopping Centre
Same attractions as most other centres,
but with a rooftop drive in.
Menlyn, Pretoria.
Tel: (011) 348 8766.
www.menlynpark.com

The Zone in Rosebank

Entertainment

Entertainment in South Africa is eclectic and mirrors the broad range of cultures and traditions of the country's people. Music and theatre often take on cross-cultural flavours, although Shakespeare and more traditionally Western plays are firm favourites in some circles. The Government has taken the development of the performing arts to heart, and the Department of Arts, Culture, Science and Technology actively promotes development of theatre, music and other disciplines. Cultural officers work throughout the country to encourage youngsters, and to assist existing groups to improve their skills in the performing arts.

Festival of the sea

BALLET AND DANCE

Traditional ballets are regularly performed in the larger centres, but less commonly so in smaller towns and rural areas. Highly talented local dancers perform in most productions, and an increasing number of international companies and dancers are visiting South Africa.

Dance takes on many forms in South Africa, and ranges from traditional Zulu and Venda dances that have been performed for centuries to various forms of modern dance, tap and classical. The best traditional dancing is often performed at cultural villages in rural parts of the country where cultural links to the past are often stronger than those in the cosmopolitan cities. At many of these performances the performers will explain the significance of each dance and what role it plays in society. Some dances are performed only at weddings, others are linked to seasonal festivals and some are just for fun.

Traditional dance is also often incorporated into music performances with band members and vocalists joining in. Ballroom dancing is extremely popular, particularly in townships. Children and adults get togged up in formal suits and dresses and compete for national awards.

THEATRE

As with music, theatre in South Africa reflects the diversity of the population. A Chekov play may be running at one theatre while a John Kani production is on at the next, and some other theatre work that falls into no particular camp will also attract audiences.

Much of South Africa's modern theatre has drawn on the experiences of the political struggle, although many playwrights are now exploring new themes.

Booking Tickets

Most theatre, opera, ballet and cinema tickets can be bought through Computicket, which has offices nation wide.

Open: Mon–Fri 9am–5pm, Sat 9am–4pm. Cash or credit card. They also handle online and telephonic booking. Nationwide call centre. Tel: 083 915 8000 or (011) 340 1000. Tel: 083 131 for information.
www.computicket.com
(Many sports match tickets can also be booked through Computicket.)

Cape Town
Artscape Theatre Centre

Theatre, ballet, opera, classical music.
DF Malan St, Foreshore.
Tel: (021) 410 9801.
www.artscape.co.za

Independent Armchair Theatre

Hosts an unusual array of comedy and other entertainment, often by young and upcoming performers.
135 Main Rd, Observatory.
Tel: (021) 447 1514.

The Baxter Theatre Centre

A Cape Town institution. Theatre, ballet, classical music.
Main Rd, Rondebosch.
Tel: (021) 685 7880.
www.baxter.co.za

Theatre on the Bay

Relaxed theatre, and you can take your drinks in with you.

1 Link St, Camps Bay.
Tel: (021) 438 3301.
www.theatreonthebay.co.za

Darling
Evita se Perron

Pieter Dirk Uys, South Africa's foremost satirist.
Darling Station, Arcadia Rd. (Darling is about an hour's drive north of Cape Town.)
Tel. (022) 492 2851.
www.evita.co.za

Durban
The Playhouse Theatre

A Durban favourite. Theatre, classical music and other shows performed in three venues.
Smith St, opposite City Hall.
Tel: (031) 369 9540.

Johannesburg
African Bank Market Theatre

A theatre with a proud history of hosting politically sensitive plays and supporting Black actors.
Newtown Precinct. Tel: (011) 832 1641.

Evita se Perron Theatre, Darling

Johannesburg Civic Theatre
Several theatres.
Loveday St, Braamfontein.
Tel: (011) 877 6800.

Liberty Theatre on the Square
Small comfortable theatre.
Nelson Mandela Square, Sandton.
Tel: (011) 883 8606.

Pretoria
State Theatre Complex
Theatre, classical music and opera in several venues.
320 Pretoria Steet, Pretoria.
Tel: (012) 392 4000.

CINEMA
The South African film industry is developing in leaps and bounds, and many international studios are using South Africa as a filming location. Most large centres hold regular film festivals, details of which are usually listed in local newspapers and on tourism authority websites.

Ster-Kinekor and Nu Metro, the two largest distributors of films in South Africa, have screens all over the country. Nearly all these cinemas are located in shopping malls. Most local newspapers publish movie listings. Some cinemas are not part of the major commercial networks and often show films not distributed on circuit.

Drive-in cinemas can still be found in some areas. The Top Star in Johannesburg is positioned on the top of a huge mine dump and has views right across the city.
Ster-Kinekor
Tel: 082 167 89. www.sterkinekor.com
Nu Metro
Tel: 086 1100 220. www.numetro.co.za

Cape Town
Imax
Amazing large-format screen, usually showing spectacular wildlife events.
Victoria and Alfred Waterfront.
Tel: (021) 419 7365.

The Labia
A favourite Cape Town venue. Fashionably laid-back, with a bar downstairs.
Orange St, Gardens.
Tel: (021) 424 5927.

The Iziko-SA National Gallery
Sometimes shows documentaries and films by local independent filmmakers. Check their listings sheets.

Cape Town City Hall

Government Ave.
Tel: (021) 456 1628.

Durban

Watch newspaper listings for shows at museums.

Johannesburg

Cinema Nouveau (9 cinemas)
Shows a variety of limited release and alternative films.
The Mall of Rosebank. Tel: 082 167 89.

MUSIC

Whatever your taste in music you should be able to find it in South Africa, and there might even be something completely new. South African music is increasingly influenced by the music of Africa, particularly West and Central Africa, and any number of bands and performers can be found experimenting with new trends.

Jazz, blues, and reggae are hugely popular amongst the majority of the population. The younger generation favour *kwaito* (the South African form of rap), trance, house and general pop. There are also a variety of venues that play good old-fashioned rock and roll. Check the local paper to see what is on offer. Occasionally rock concerts featuring international and local stars are hosted at sports stadiums or indoor arenas.

Opera and classic music are often performed in the larger cities, sometimes in the grand old buildings built as city halls. Theatre and opera-goers usually dress fairly smartly but leave their best clothes for opening nights. In clubs people wear whatever they feel like or whatever they think their friends think they should wear!

Cape Town
Cape Town City Hall
Classical music and opera in grand surroundings.
Darling St.
Tel: (021) 410 9809.
www.capephilharmonic.org.za

Green Dolphin

Live Jazz and dining.
V&A Waterfront. Tel: (021) 421 7471.
www.greendolphin.co.za
Open: all week.

46664 poster on buliding

Mannenberg's Jazz Café
Live jazz and dining. Music usually from
8.30pm.
Clock Towers Centre, V&A Waterfront.
Tel: (021) 421 5639. Open: all week.

Durban
Catalina Theatre
Operettas, classic music.
Wilsons Wharf. Tel: (031) 305 6889.

Durban City Hall
Home of the KZN Philharmonic
Orchestra. Classical music and other
concerts.
Smith St. Tel. (031) 369 9438.
www.kznpo.co.za

Thousands flock to the summer evening concerts
at the Kirstenbosch National Botanical Gardens

Copyright: South African Tourism

Johannesburg
Kippies Jazz International
Famous Johannesburg jazz club.
Market Theatre Complex.
Tel. (011) 833 3316.
www.kippies.co.za

Johannesburg City Hall
Classical music and other performances.
President St.
Johannesburg Computicket.
Tel. (011) 789 2733.

Kilimanjaro
Very trendy supper-dance club.
Melrose Arch, Melrose.
Tel. (011) 214 4300.

Linder Auditorium
Classical music and theatre.
Wits Education Campus, St Andrews Rd,
Parktown.
Bookings through Computicket.

OPEN-AIR VENUES
Cape Town
Kirstenbosch Summer Sunset
Concerts: Jazz, classical music, choirs.
Winter visitor centre hosts indoor
concerts weekly.
Kirstenbosch National Botanical Gardens,
Rhodes Dr, Newlands.
Tel: (021) 799 8783.
www.nbi.ac.za

Oude Libertas Amphitheatre
Classical music and dance.
Adam Tas Rd, Stellenbosch.
Tel: (021) 809 1111.
www.oudelibertas.co.za

Durban
Botanical Gardens
Sometimes hosts outdoors concerts.
Tel: (031) 201 1303.
Sydenham Rd, Musgrave.

Johannesburg
Walter Sisulu National Botanical Gardens
Popular classical music in the gardens on summer afternoons.
Malcom Rd, Poortview, Roodepoort.
Open: 8am–5pm all year. Admission charge.
Tel: (011) 958 1750 or 958 0529.
www.nbi.ac.za

BARS AND PUBS
As is to be expected in a place like South Africa, there are a huge number of bars and pubs. Nearly all offer food and drink, but in a sports-mad country it's the establishments that screen live sports matches that get really packed.

In these pubs and bars, most of the important international rugby, cricket and soccer matches are screened live, and the atmosphere in the better venues is second only to being at the game. The partisan fans welcome anyone who enjoys sport.

Golf, Formula One racing and English soccer are also regularly screened, as are special events including the Olympics and the Tour de France. The more seriously sports-oriented pubs show the matches on big screens.

Cape Town
The Fireman's Arms
Fun 1906 vintage bar with great atmosphere.

25 Mechau St, City Bowl.
Tel: (021) 419 1513.

The Sports Café
Screens endless international sport.
Upper Level, Victoria Wharf.
Tel: (021) 419 5558.

Durban
Billy the Bum's
A venue favoured by a generally young and affluent crowd.
504 Windemere Rd.
Tel: (031) 303 1988.

Johannesburg
The Grand Slam
A huge venue that gets packed with hundreds of people during important games.
Corner Witkoppen Rd and Sycamore Dr.
Tel: (011) 454 3700.

Billy the Bum's
Owned by the same group as the Durban pub. Similar crowd, same sports.
Pineslopes Centre, Witkoppen Rd.
Tel: (011) 465 2621.

Listings
Check local daily newspapers for listings sections. The national *Mail&Guardian* newspaper, published Fridays, gives excellent coverage to major cities. The *Mail&Guardian* also as a very good entertainment section on its website: *www.mg.co.za*

Most regional tourism websites have links to 'what's on', in their areas.

vimming race, KwaZulu-Natal

Copyright: South African Tourism

THE BIG EVENTS
e most important events on
ica's sporting calendar attract
ands of participants and are
iggest of their kind anywhere.
4,000 athletes participate in the
rades Marathon raced over 89km
tween Durban and
burg. Held on 16th June, it is
many as one of the world's
ra-marathons'.

us Cycle race is one of the largest in
Every year in April, some 34,000
w the spectacularly scenic 106km
course that treats participants to
iews of the mountains, sea and

dmar Mile in KwaZulu Natal is another
sporting event where thousands of
race across the Midmar Dam.

South African Sport

When Bafana Bafana ('The Boys'), South Africa's soccer team, loses a match, the event immediately sparks radio talk show discussions, letters to newspapers and heated debate in bars, on busses and on street corners. Fire the coach! Fire the administrators! Ask the government to intervene!

South Africans don't like losing, and the response is similar if the national rugby team does badly at the World Cup or the cricket team does not meet expectations. Most sporting nations are passionate about their favourite team, but in South Africa losses and victories take on a special edge because sport here often has a political sub-plot.

For decades Black players were barred from participating in top teams, and sports administrators are still trying to ensure that equal opportunities are offered to all in terms of training, facilities and financial backing.

Long-denied international competition because of sports boycotts imposed in protest against apartheid, sports fans are eager for success, and woe betide the teams that don't fulfil these aspirations. At the top end, sports stadiums and facilities are world class, and the nation has hosted the Rugby World Cup, Cricket World Cup, Africa Cup of Nations (soccer), the Africa Games (athletics) and several internationally important golf tournaments during the last 10 years.

Soccer is by far South Africa's most popular sport. Across the nation, television and, particularly in poorer and rural areas, radio, keep millions up to date on important matches, both local and international. As is the case with soccer matches anywhere, attending a big match is a raucous affair and fans, some in fancy dress, whistle and blow bugles to urge on their team.

Many teams have imaginative names, and the Dangerous Darkies (humourously named if politically incorrect), usually get thrashed by Kaiser Chiefs, the country's most popular team. Kaiser Chiefs have a fan club that stretches far into Africa, and a game against arch-rivals Orlando Pirates (both teams are based in Soweto) is one of the highlights of the season and is treated with the same frenzy as a World Cup Final.

Rugby fans are no less passionate, and the national team has a hundred-year-old reputation of being one of the toughest and best in the world, a

South African fast bowler Makhaya Ntini

Copyright: South African Tourism

their local is by f and imate s and large have g and

ost provinces have world-class urses.

orehensive list of all the sporting in South Africa can be found on bsite of the **South African Sports** ission.

12) 677 9746. www.sasc.org.za ebsite includes contact numbers, led meetings or matches, officials enues. It is particularly good for g plan which events to attend.

Government's **Department of** ts and Recreation also has a useful ite: www.srsa.gov.za 012) 465 5506.

tact details for major sports:

etics South Africa (011) 880 5800. v.athleticssa.co.za

uestrian Association of South Africa (012) 803 9351. w.thsinfo.co.za

Copyright: South African Tourism

Copyright: South African Tourism

world's top **golfers**, although the sport has fairly limited appeal because of the cost of playing the game regularly.

As befits a country with lots of sunshine, **watersports** are widespread. Many people water-ski on inland lakes and dams on weekends, much to the annoyance of others participating in the far more leisurely, but hugely popular, fishing. Popular **ball sports** include basketball, field hockey, bowls, netball and tennis. South Africans also enjoy **gambling**, and most large cities host regular horse race meetings.

reputation that is sometimes hard to live up to in the demanding world of professional sport.

Traditionally dominated by White Afrikaans speakers, rugby is changing its profile to be more representative. One of its defining moments was Nelson Mandela holding the World Cup with victorious captain, Francois Pienaar, in 1995.

Cricket is another sport in which South Africa has excelled and a sport that is also changing its racial profile to become more representative. Athletics and boxing are also popular, and South Africans have performed well on the international stage. Many athletes participate in the professional athletic circuits in Europe and Asia.

The country's long-distance **runners** are particularly successful, and a large number of marathons are organised every year. South Africans have consistently been listed among the

Opposite: Fancourt Golf Course, near George, Garden Route
Above: Soccer supporters

SOCCER WORLD CUP

South Africa will host the 2010 Soccer World Cup, one of the world's most popular sporting events.

The tournament attracts hundreds of thousands of fans, and is expected to provide a huge boost to the South African economy with a simultaneous increase in other forms of tourism. The country has many excellent soccer and rugby stadiums (which are often also used for soccer matches) and others will be renovated to cope with the expected influx of visitors.

Soccer is the most popular sport in Africa where South Africa's hosting of the Cup is regarded as particularly prestigious.

Children

South Africa's good climate and open spaces make it a pleasant place for children to visit. In the cities, many teenagers hang out in shopping malls where they can go to the movies, chat with their friends or get something to eat in safety. In many cases the 'kids culture' is very American, and Hollywood movies, television, pop stars and even fast food often have an American orientation.

A youngster has fun at an open-air fair

Travelling with Small Children

All the essentials from disposable nappies to DVDs are widely available. Bear in mind that if you are travelling, distances between locations can be very long, so carry books and games. Many South African parents resort to allowing their children to play endless cellular-phone games to ease the boredom.

Playing in the sea at Camps Bay

There are excellent service stations on most major routes, and these have well-looked-after toilets, fast-food outlets and general stores. Some even have small gardens where children can use up surplus energy.

Many South African fast food and family restaurants have children's menus.

Swimming

Currents along the South African coast can be powerful and unpredictable. Never allow children to swim unattended. Many more popular beaches have lifeguards, but the coastline is long, and it is not possible to patrol it all. Some beaches have tidal pools that make for safe swimming. Make sure that children refresh their sun block regularly.

National Parks

All the national parks are well equipped to cater for children, and many rest camps have playgrounds and swimming pools. All the camps at the major parks are fenced and are quite safe. Do not let children, or anyone else, feed the

Walter Sisulu National Botanical Gardens

monkeys or baboons.

In some of the larger parks, hyaenas have learnt that some people throw supper scraps over the fence and make nightly patrols to see what food has been left out. Do not feed them and don't let children go up to the fence with food in their hands. Hyaenas have immensely powerful jaws.

Not all private game lodges allow children under the age of 16 or, in some cases, 14.

Hotels

Some hotels can arrange a babysitting service. Both local and satellite TV services have a selection of children's programmes.

There are a wide range of entertainment parks, playgrounds and children-orientated activities available in most cities and towns. Many special activities and entertainments are organised over the Christmas and Easter holidays. Tourism authorities will be only too happy to tell you what has been arranged in their area.

Kleinmond Estuary, Western Cape

Food and Drink

South Africans are just as fond of local dishes as they are of Italian, Chinese, Indian and other cuisines from around the globe. A quick glance at the supermarket shelves reveals the multi-cultural nature of South African eating habits and, particularly in the cities, most people will find something that suits their preferred diet. Meat features prominently in many meals, but although it is cheap by Western standards, it is regarded as a luxury by poor people. Chicken is extremely popular as an affordable form of protein.

Good weather makes for pleasurable outdoor eating

South African Specialities

Biltong is more than a snack food for many South Africans; it's almost a cult item. Connoisseurs will debate the fat content, composition of the spices and moisture content. It's like wine tasting for beer-drinking sports fans.

Biltong, savoury dried meat, is sold all over South Africa. It is eaten while having a drink in a bar, watching a rugby match on television or pretty much at anytime someone feels like a salty snack. It is usually made from beef or game animals, including kudu and eland. Ostrich meat is also used.

Strips of raw meat are usually dipped in vinegar, coated in ground coriander seed, black pepper and salt and then hung in a cool dry place to cure. Under the right circumstances, it is ready after a few days and is cut into thin slices. The early Dutch settlers originally used the recipe as a means of preserving meat.

Bobotie

Bobotie is ground lamb flavoured with turmeric, cinnamon and other spices covered with a form of custard and baked in the oven. It is usually served with yellow rice, raisins and stewed fruits.

Boerewors

This is a homemade sausage filled with a variety of meats and spices. *Boerewors* (farmers' sausage) is a favourite among many South Africans.

Bunny chow

Bunny chow is a Durban phenomenon. A half loaf of square-shaped bread is hollowed out and filled with meat or vegetables. The inside of the bread is used to scoop the curry out.

Koeksisters

Koeksisters are favourites among Afrikaans-speaking people, and are made from fried dough dipped in very sweet syrup.

Cuisine from around the world is popular with diners across South Africa

THE BRAAI

In simple terms, a *braai* is a barbecue where meat, poultry, fish or vegetables, or all of them, are grilled over an open fire.

The braai is a whole cultural experience that is popular in all sectors of the population. As with the 'potjie' everyone has their own idea as to the perfect recipe and method, but in the end the braai serves the same purpose for all – it's a great way to socialise, relax and enjoy good weather. Beer, wine and other drinks usually accompany the event.

You will find South Africans having a braai in the lush gardens of Camps Bay in Cape Town, the dusty streets of Mhlabathini in Zululand or in the rest camps at the Kruger National Park. Almost everyone 'braais'.

Mealies

Mealies (maize on the cob) roasted over an open brazier are a popular snack food for many South Africans. They can often be bought on city street corners particularly in Johannesburg, Soweto and surrounding areas. They are usually quite crisp and chewy.

Mopane worms

Mopane worms are an acquired, peppery taste, but worth a try. Mopane worms are the caterpillar of the emperor moth and are dried in the sun. They are very nutritious and are eaten as a snack or with *pap*. They are often sold on the streets of Johannesburg, Pretoria and Pholokwane and are sometimes served in restaurants that specialise in African food.

Pap and vleis

Pap en vleis (firm porridge and meat) is the favourite food of many South Africans. The meat is usually barbecued or grilled and the *'pap'* is a firm porridge made from de-husked maze and served with gravy. *Pap* is as popular amongst Zulu- and Xhosa-speaking people as it is in Afrikaans-speaking communities. In various forms it is found throughout southern and east Africa. In Zulu it is called *phutu*, amongst Zimbabweans it is *sadza* and in parts of Zambia it is called *ntshima* – in short, most people eat it. Some people prefer it moist, some dry; others like it with sour milk and others with gravy.

Potjiekos

Potjiekos is meat and vegetables cooked in a heavy cast-iron three-legged pot. The pot *(potjie)* is placed over open coals and the stew is left to simmer for hours. Everyone has their own recipe and method and will stoutly defend their way of cooking a *potjie* (pronounced 'poyt-key') as being the only way to do so.

Prawns Peri-peri

Prawns Peri-peri is a recipe brought to South Africa by Portuguese visitors from Mozambique. Pawns are coated in olive oil, lemon juice, garlic and peri-peri (hot ground chillies), and then grilled.

Sosaties

Sosaties (kebabs) are skewered lamb, beef or even vegetables.

Smoorsnoek

Smoorsnoek is a typical Cape Malay dish made with smoked snoek (a large predatory fish similar to a barracuda), chilli, onions, potatoes and sometimes tomato. It is usually served with some form of chutney or jam, and the snoek should be smoked over oak.

Waterblommetjie breedie

Waterblommetjie breedie (water lily stew) is a form of stew made from lamb and the buds of indigenous water lily. It is a speciality of the Western Cape.

WHERE TO EAT AND DRINK
Price guide:

* = main course up to R65
** = up to R85
*** = over R85

Cape Town
Blues**

Trendy seafood restaurant right over the road from Camps Bay Beach.
Victoria Rd, Camps Bay.
Tel: (021) 438 2040.

Cape to Cuba**

Friendly and fun, with a view of the harbour. Good seafood and old Havana décor.
Main Rd, Kalk Bay.
Tel: (021) 788 1566.

Cape Colony***

Top-class, refined restaurant with formal menu and excellent service.
Mount Nelson Hotel, Gardens.
Tel: (021) 483 1198.

Buitenverwagting***

Old favourite on lovely wine farm. Great place to spend an afternoon or for dinner.

South Africa's good weather is ideal for outdoor festivals and fairs

Cape restaurateurs make the most of the wonderful scenery and great location

Klein Constantia Rd, Constantia.
Tel: (021) 794 3522.

Downs*

Good place for a drink while watching the sun set over Hout Bay.
1 Beach Rd, Hout Bay.
Tel: (021) 790 1876.

Durban
Aka**

Small innovative restaurant with daily change in menu. All cooking is done by the owner.
Vause Centre, Vause Rd, Musgrave.
Tel: (031) 201 0767.

The Havana Grill**

Lively grill house with excellent meat and seafood dishes.
Shop U2, Suncoast Casino.
Tel. (031) 337 1305.

Naked*

Indoors and outdoors eating. Fashionable and imaginative menu.
9th Ave, Windermere.
Tel: (031) 312 0755.

Royal Hotel*–***

Several busy bars.
Smith St, opposite City Hall.
Tel: (031) 333 6000.

Florida Road

A variety of cafes on bars on this busy street are good places for a cocktail or drink.
Florida Rd, Durban.

Franschhoek
Le Quartier Francais**

Lovely al fresco dining, but warm inside in winter. Skilfully run with a top-class reputation.
Main Rd, Franschhoek.
Tel: (021) 876 3105.

Johannesburg
Yum***

One of the top restaurants in the country – designer salmon, calamari and rump steak. Relaxed atmosphere.
12 Gleneagles Rd, Greenside.
Tel: (011) 486 1645.

Kapitan's Café*

Wonderful curries and atmosphere in a restaurant once frequented by Nelson

Mandela.
1a Kort St.
Tel: (011) 834 8048.
Daytime only.

The Grill House**
Top-class steak, lamb and seafood. Try
Katzy's next door for a late-night drink.
32a Cradock Ave, inside Rosebank Mall.
Tel: (011) 880 3945.

Gramadoelas**
The best-established traditional South
African food restaurant in
Johannesburg. Also dishes from
elsewhere.
Market Theatre, Newtown.
Tel: (011) 838 6960.

The Turtle Creek Winery**
Great for a drink under the oak trees in
summer. Nice fire inside in winter.
12 Wierda Valley Rd.
Tel: (011) 884 0465.

Knysna
The Oystercatcher*
Oysters fresh from the sea and a great
view of the lagoon.
Small Craft Harbour, Knysna.
Tel: (044) 382 6943.

Pretoria
La Madeleine's***
Top-class Mediterranean-style
restaurant, popular with politicians and
diplomats.
122 Priory Rd, Lynwood Ridge.
Tel: (012) 361 3667.

Stellenbosch
Spier Estate***

Cape Malay buffet and other meals on a
wine state with lovely gardens. Café too.
Baden Powell Dr, near Stellenbosch.
Tel: (021) 809 1100.

Tulbagh
Paddagang Wine House*
Traditional Cape menu includes smoked
snoek pate and sometimes
waterblommetjie breedie.
23 Church St, Tulbagh.
Tel: (023) 230 0242.

EATING OUT

Restaurants in South Africa are similar to
those found throughout the western
world, but it must be remembered that there
are strict anti-smoking laws that allow smoking
in designated areas only. Most restaurants,
particularly more expensive establishments,
enforce these laws.

Nearly all good restaurants, excluding a few
which are *Halaal*, serve alcohol. If you intend
taking your own wine, it is worth checking
beforehand about corkage charges, because in
some instances these are high.

If any item on the menu is marked SQ, ask
the price before ordering – these dishes tend
to be expensive.

If you intend visiting a restaurant and the
weather is good, which is often, even in
winter, ask about outside seating – many
South Africans take good weather for granted
and forget to mention outside eating areas.

Only a few dishes are truly indigenous to South Africa, and the country's culinary tradition is derived from the cuisine of a variety of countries. Many recipes have been adapted over the centuries with the inclusion of local ingredients and the introduction of innovative cooking methods.

Indigenous Cuisine

Maize forms the staple diet of the vast majority of South Africans. It is usually prepared in the form of *pap*, a stiff porridge made from ground de-husked maize.

It is served with meat or vegetables, but in poorer homes meat is something of a treat. *Pap* is also eaten with *maas* (milk curds).

Samp (whole de-husked maize) and kidney beans is another popular dish. Sorghum, a cereal indigenous to Africa,

sweet potatoes, onions, pumpkins and a variety of wild plants are also commonly used. Wild spinach is used to make a stew called *morogo*, which is often spiced with a chilli-based relish.

Many restaurants in the townships serve these meals regularly, and more and more upmarket restaurants specialising in African foods are creating stylised versions.

Other Cuisines

Many South African dishes have their origins elsewhere in the world. Dutch, English, Indian and Malay people have all contributed to the style and flavour. The Malay slaves who worked in the kitchens of Dutch settlers helped introduce Indonesian sweet and sour dishes, pickles and chutney.

The Indian population in KwaZulu-Natal brought curries, samoosas and nan bread with them, and some English-speaking South Africans still enjoy a Sunday lunch of roast beef complete with Yorkshire pudding.

Many of the dishes have been adapted over time and have become truly South African products.

Restaurants

South Africa has an enormous variety of restaurants offering international cuisine from around the globe. Italian, Indian, Portuguese, Greek, Chinese and Japanese food is widely available. French cuisine is also popular, particularly in restaurants based in the winelands.

Johannesburg has a growing Chinese population and, in the Bruma area, there are more Chinese restaurants than any other.

Meat forms the basis of many meals among those who can afford it. There are any number of grill houses that prepare excellent steaks, rack of lamb or pork spare ribs. Fresh seafood is usually available in seafood restaurants along the coast and in Johannesburg, where restaurateurs have fresh fish, oysters, crayfish (a species of rock lobster) and prawns flown in regularly.

Several restaurants specialise in venison, and springbok, eland and kudu are often available, as well as game birds including guinea fowl. Most restaurants cater for vegetarians, but some with more skill than others. Of course there are any number of fast-food outlets serving burgers, chicken or fish in forms familiar all over the world.

Drink

The country's favourite alcoholic drink is beer, most of which is drunk in the form of bottled lager, but traditional sorghum beer, or *mahewu*, is also hugely popular.

Wine is widely available, and many South Africans pride themselves on their knowledge of the local industry.

In KwaZulu-Natal, cane spirits is a popular addition to cola, and brandy is a favourite in Limpopo and the Western Cape. For the bold there is *mampoer* or *witblits*, which has a very high alcohol content and is made of just about anything, but usually grains or fruit. Treat with caution!

Opposite: Whisky, cocktails, or even beer – you can usually find your favourite tipple in most South African bars
Left: Top South African chefs are highly skilled and produce world-class food

Hotels and Accommodation

South Africa has a wide array of hotels, bed and breakfasts (B&Bs), self-catering apartments and other forms of accommodation. They range from the ultra-luxurious hotels and game lodges to self-catering apartments where you do your own cooking. The South African tourism industry has grown by leaps and bounds over the past few years, and one can usually find good accommodation even in the smaller towns.

Accommodation for all tastes

South African Tourism and the regional tourism authorities all have excellent websites listing accommodation. All the tourism offices are happy to help tourists find accommodation no matter what the price range.

Hotels

South African hotels are rated on a star basis with five stars denoting 'outstanding' or 'luxury' and, at the bottom end of the scale, one star indicating a no-frills establishment.

Some hotels and B&Bs choose not to be rated but still offer excellent value for money and service. The objective of the national grading scheme is to assist in the improvement of the overall quality of accommodation and services in South Africa. The aim is not to police or impose strict and inflexible guidelines on graded establishments.

Luxury or outstanding hotels are world class and offer everything a guest would expect of a top-of-the-range establishment. Many are in the larger cities, but there has been a profusion of smaller 'boutique hotels' built recently in the prettier parts of the country.

Sandton Sun Hotel

Granny Mouse B&B

Many of the private game lodges fall into this category. They offer personalised service and top-class cooking, as well as showing off the wild residents of the area.

Top-of-the-range hotels in cities include The Table Bay in Cape Town, The Royal in Durban and The Westcliff in Johannesburg. Top country lodges include Walkersons near Dullstroom and the Coach House near Tzaneen. Sabi Sabi and Londolozi are just two of the many luxury game lodges.

Two- and three-star hotels tend to be comfortable and good value for money. These may also include some of the less exclusive game lodges. This category also includes some of the chain and business hotels.

B&Bs

There are large numbers of B&Bs in all the major tourist areas. Some are in people's homes where the host treats tourists as members of the family, and others are entirely self-contained cottages or houses. Most hosts will arrange dinner if requested.

Breakfasts are usually fruit, cereal and toast or bacon and eggs.

There are also B&Bs in some townships, and staying there provides an insight on a very different world to what one would experience in a soulless hotel. All the tourism authorities have lists of good B&Bs.

Guesthouses tend to be converted houses or stand-alone buildings where the owner does not stay in the dwelling.

Accommodation in Private Game Reserves

Most private game reserves charge more than national parks and have more luxurious accommodation. (Guests also travel in open vehicles with professional guides.)

All meals are usually provided. At private game reserves everything from making tea to cooking supper and spotting animals is usually done for guests by the staff.

Accommodation in National Parks and Game Reserves

Clean and comfortable chalets are the standard accommodation in most national parks and game reserves. In most cases, guests cater for themselves, and the chalets are equipped with a fridge, stove or hotplate, cutlery, crockery and kitchen utensils.

They almost inevitably all have braai facilities for outdoor cooking too. Most camps supply utensils and crockery, but always confirm this when booking. Most of these chalets have their own bathroom, but in some instances there are shared ablution blocks. They are

Backpackers' sign, Hogsback, Eastern Cape

national parks are provided outdoors with electric hotplates and hot water available. The weather is usually warm enough to make cooking outdoors a pleasant experience. In places like the Kruger National Park, it is the preferred way of preparing supper.

(Don't leave dirty plates or bits of food lying around, because there are many small animals that will eat the scraps, often to their detriment.)

usually spotlessly clean.

Many game reserves also offer safari-tent accommodation. Safari tents are large tents equipped with proper beds. Some have showers installed, and some have their own cooking facilities.

Communal cooking facilities in most

Backpackers' Accommodation

There are backpacker lodges in most of the bigger cities and in some smaller towns too, particularly along the Garden Route and elsewhere along the coast. It is not advisable to sleep on beaches or in parks.

Health Spas

There are a number of exclusive health

Pakamisa Private Game Reserve

Self-catering accomodation in Paternoster

spas set in beautiful countryside. Most have swimming pools, some have tennis courts and there is often good mountain biking or hiking in the area. The spas cater for a wide range of taste and expenditure.

Rented Accommodation
There are self-catering, serviced apartments available for short-term rents. Some people also rent out their entire homes over holiday periods, which is an option that can be considered if tourists are travelling in a small party. Prices have increased in recent years. Tourism authorities will assist in finding rented accommodation.

Caravanning and Camper Vans
There are many caravan parks throughout South Africa. There are also beautiful sites in nature reserves and resorts. All are equipped with ablution blocks, open-air cooking facilities and electrical outlets. Several companies have camper vans to rent.

Farm Stays
There are many B&Bs on working farms throughout the country, and spending a day or two at one is a good way to learn a bit about country life in South Africa.

Camping
Most game reserves have campsites suitable for pitching tents. Nearly all have ablution blocks and outdoor cooking facilities.

To Find Accommodation
South Africa Tourism
Tel: (011) 895 3000.
www.southafrica.net
Please also see websites listed under each regional tourism authority.
Also try:
Tel: (031) 262 1166.
www.wheretostay.co.za

South Africa has no fewer than 11 official languages, but most people manage to communicate through a combination of Zulu, English or Afrikaans. A large number of South Africans are multilingual and speak as many as five different languages regularly. Most people in South African business and tourism communicate in English. Signage is also in English. Major newspapers are published in English, Afrikaans and Zulu, and most literature is written in English. French is spoken by some migrants from Central and West Africa.

Place Names

Throughout South Africa, many cities, towns, rivers and mountains have names in Afrikaans, Zulu, Sotho and other local languages. Many of the Afrikaans names are derived from the original Dutch, and make reference to animals or natural phenomenon, such as snow or the colour of rocks. A lot of the names are an interesting, if rather sad, record of the former distribution of wild animals, many of which were hunted to the point of local extinction.

Since the 1994 elections, the names of some towns, rivers and other landmarks that formerly had Afrikaans names have been replaced with ones from Black languages. Warmbaths, north of Pretoria, is now known as Bela Bela, but both names refer to the hot springs there. Pietersburg, originally named after a Voortrekker leader, is now called Polokwane after a local chief.

Some Zulu place names are prefixed with *kwa* which means 'place of', as in Kwambonambi ('place of the Bonambi clan'). *Kwa* is often used as a prefix to the names of rivers, mountains or plains.

Common Terms

| **English:** Yes | **Afrikaans:** Ja |
| **Xhosa:** Ewe | **Zulu:** Yebo |

| **English:** No | **Afrikaans:** Nee |
| **Xhosa:** Hayi | **Zulu:** Cha |

English:	**Afrikaans:**
How are you?	Hoe gaan dit?
Xhosa: Kunjani?	**Zulu:** Kunjani?

| **English:** Thank you | **Afrikaans:** Dankie |
| **Xhosa:** Enkosi | **Zulu:** Ngiyabonga |

| **English:** How much? | **Afrikaans:** Hoeveel? |
| **Xhosa:** Yimalini? | **Zulu:** Yimalini? |

English:	**Afrikaans:**
Good morning	Goeie more
Xhosa: Molo	**Zulu:** Sawubona

English:	**Afrikaans:**
Where is the	Waar is die
post office/bank	poskantoor/bank/
/hotel?	hotel?
Xhosa:	**Zulu:**
Iphi iposi/ibhanki	Iphi iposi /ibhange
/ihotele?	/ihhotele?

Geographical Features (Afrikaans)

Rivier – river.
Spruit – spring.
Berg – mountain.
Vlakte – plains.

Animals (Afrikaans)

Bok – buck (as in springbuck or springbok).
Buffel – buffalo (Buffelspruit means 'buffalo spring').
Kameelperd – giraffe.
Leeu – lion.
Olifant – elephant (also spelt *oliphant*).
Renoster – rhinoceros.
Qwagga – a creature similar to a zebra, shot to extinction.
Seekoei – hippopotamus (directly translated means 'sea cow').
Tier – leopard (directly translated means tiger, but is a misnomer).
Wolve – hyaena (directly translated means wolves, also a misnomer).

Other Afrikaans Names Commonly Used:

Dorp – village, as in Krugersdorp, 'Kruger's village'.
Strand – beach, as in Bloubergstrand.
Klein – small, as in Klein Constantia.
Mond – river mouth, as in Kleinmond.
Sneeu – snow.
Kloof – a gorge or cutting through a mountain, as in Magoebaskloof (kloof of Magoeba, former chief in Limpopo).

Bosch – bush, or wild area, as in Stellenbosch.
Swart – black.
Rooi – red.
Blou – blue.

Other Names Derived From Traditions, Plants or Aspects of Life

Tzaneen, in Limpopo, comes from Pedi, and means 'the place where people gather'.

Hluhluwe (KwaZulu-Natal) derives its name from the Zulu word for a common thorny creeper.

One of the nicest names is that of Ixopo, in southern KwaZulu-Natal, which earns its name from the onomatopoeic Zulu description of 'the sound of a cow's foot being pulled from mud'.

Below: Hippopotamus – *Seekoei*

Practical Guide

ARRIVING
Documents

Visitors must hold a valid passport, endorsed with a visa if required. For information on passport and visa requirements, contact your local passport office or the diplomatic or consular representative of the South African Government. Proof is required that you can support yourself in South Africa. If you do not have a return ticket, you must show that you have the means to buy one.

By Air

International airports at Johannesburg, Cape Town and Durban have regular scheduled flights from all over the world. South African Airways (SAA) is partly owned by the state. Airport Tax is included in the price of the air ticket. These taxes are levied for both international and domestic flights.

Airline Offices
Air France
Tel: (011) 770 1601.
www.airfrance.co.za

British Airways
Tel: (011) 441 8600 or
toll free 086 001 1747.
www.british-airways.co.za

Kulula
Tel: toll free 086 158 58 52.
www.kulula.com
Domestic routes only.

Johannesburg International Airport is modern, and compares with the best anywhere

Johannesburg is linked to airports all over the world

Lufthansa
Tel: (011) 484 4711 or
toll free 086 184 2538.
www.lufhthansa.com

Nationwide Airlines
Tel: toll free 0861 737 737.
www.flynationwide.co.za
Domestic routes only.

Qantas
Tel: (011) 441 8550.
www.qantas.com

South African Airways (SAA)
Tel: (011) 978 1111.
www.flysaa.com

Virgin Atlantic
Tel: (011) 340 3500.
www.virgin-atlantic.com

For other airlines, see the telephone directory.

Airports
The main airports are:

Johannesburg International (25km east of Johannesburg)
Serving both Johannesburg and Pretoria, this is a busy international terminus with extensive duty-free facilities. Scheduled bus services are available between airport and city centres, taxis are readily on hand, and car rental companies are represented. *General enquiries. Tel: (011) 921 6262.*

Cape Town Airport
A scheduled bus service connects airport and city centre (about 20km) at regular intervals. Taxis are available and all the major car-hire companies are represented.
Flight details. Tel: (021) 934 0407.

Durban Airport
A regular bus service connects airport and city centre (about 20km/12,4 miles). Taxis are available and all major car hire companies are represented.
Flight details. Tel: (031) 408 1155.

By Land
South Africa has land borders with Namibia, Botswana, Zimbabwe, Mozambique, Swaziland and Lesotho. All are open at the time of writing. Visas may be required by some nationalities. Most border posts are not open 24 hours a day.

By Sea
A number of shipping companies provide cargo/passenger services linking South Africa and Europe. Various cruise liners visit South African ports from time to time.
    The Safmarine Shipping Company

has space for 12 passengers in six double cabins on each of the 'Big White' container ships that travel between Cape Town and Tilbury, UK. The trip takes 14–16 days.
Tel: (021) 525 2470.
www.safmarine.co.za

The **RMS St Helena** travels between Cape Town, the Island of St Helena and Cardiff several times a year.
Andrew Wier Shipping
Tel: (021) 425 1165 or UK 207 816 4800.
www.rms-st-helena.com

Permitted Imports
Currency
Only R5,000 in South African Reserve Bank notes can be imported, while unlimited foreign currency and traveller's cheques are allowed, provided they are declared on arrival. Foreign passport holders may not take out more foreign currency than they declared on arrival.

Drugs
Narcotics and habit-forming drugs are prohibited.

Duty Free Allowance
400 cigarettes, 250g of tobacco and 50 cigars, one litre of spirits, two litres of wine, 50ml of perfume and 250ml of eau de toilette. Also gifts, souvenirs and all other goods to the value of R500. No person under 18 is entitled to the alcohol or tobacco allowance. Duty is levied at 20 per cent thereafter.

CAMPING AND CARAVANNING
Both camping and caravanning are exceptionally good value *(see 'Hotels and*

Accommodation' on pp166–9). The local tourism bureau will supply information about sites.

CHILDREN
See pp156–7.

CLIMATE
See charts and Geography and Climate on pp6–9.

CONVERSION TABLES
See p188.

CRIME
See p32.

DRIVING
Car Rental
Although theft and damage insurance should be bought when renting the car, most companies have a minimum 'excess' charge, which is the amount you will have to pay if the car is damaged or stolen. The excess also applies to the radio/tape.

You can agree to pay a larger amount for insurance, which reduces the excess. Ask about the excess when booking the car. Look for rentals that offer free daily mileage if travelling long distance. Ask if the company has any special deals on offer. You need a valid driver's licence and sometimes a minimum age is specified.

Avis
Toll free in South Africa.
Tel: 0861 02 1111.
International calls.
Tel: + 27 11 394 5433.
www.avis.com

A wide range of car rental companies have offices at all major airports

Budget
Toll free in South Africa.
Tel: 0861 01 6622.
International calls. Tel: +27 11 394 2905.
www.budget.co.za

Europcar
Toll free in South Africa.
Tel: 0800 01 1344.
International calls. Tel: +27 11 394 1406.
www.europcar.co.za

Imperial
Toll free in South Africa.
Tel: 0861 13 1000.
International calls.
Tel: +27 11 394 4020.
www.imperialcarrental.co.za

Maui
Camper van rental.
All calls. Tel: (011) 396 1445.
www.maui.co.za

Sani Van Rental
Toll free in South Africa
Tel: 0861 00 2111.
International calls.
Tel: +27 11 362 2111.
www.sani.co.za

Tempest/Sixt
Toll free in South Africa.
Tel: 0860 03 1666.
International calls.
Tel: +27 11 396 1080.
www.tempestcarhire.co.za

Thrifty
Toll free in South Africa.
Tel: 0861 00 211.
International calls.
Tel: +27 11 362 2111.
www.thrifty.co.za

On the Road
The road network is excellent, and you

drive on the left. The speed limit in built-up areas is 60kph, on secondary roads l00kph and on freeways 120kph, unless otherwise indicated.

Traffic laws are strictly enforced: seat belts are compulsory; carry your driving licence; do not drive under the influence of alcohol. Before your departure, check with the Automobile Association (AA) in your country whether an International Driving Permit is needed to drive in South Africa.

Filling stations are plentiful on major routes, infrequent on others. On major routes most are open 24 hours a day and have excellent facilities including fast food restaurants and toilets. Most others are open 7am–7pm. Pay for fuel with cash – credit cards are not accepted (some banks issue special 'petrocards'). *For expert advice contact the* **Automobile Association of South Africa,** *Tel: 0800 010101 (tollfree). Head office: AA House, 66 De Korte St, Braamfontein 2001. Tel: (011) 407 1000.*

South Africa has an excellent electricity network

ELECTRICITY
Power is delivered at 220/230 volts AC, 50Hz. Sockets accept round two-prong plugs. Adaptors are available at stores in the cities and bigger towns.

EMBASSIES AND CONSULATES
South African consulates in selected countries are listed below.
For further information go the website of the **Department of Foreign Affairs**. *Tel: (012) 351 1000. www.dfa.gov.za*

Overseas
Australia
SA High Commission
Corner Rhodes Pl. and State Circle, Yarralumla, Canberra, ACT 2600. Tel: (02) 62 73 2424. www.rsa.emb.gov.au

Canada
SA Consulate
15 Sussex Drive, Ottawa, Ontario, K1M 1M8. Tel: (613) 744 0330. www.rsafrica@southafrica-canada.com

Germany
South African Embassy
Tiergarten St 18, 10785 Berlin. Tel: (30) 220 730. www.suedafrika.org

United Kingdom
South African High Commission
South Africa House
Trafalgar Square. London WC2N5DP.

Tel: (207) 7451 7283.
info@saembassy.org

United States of America
Los Angeles:
SA Consulate
6300 Wilshire Boulevard, Suite 600,
Los Angeles, CA 90048.
Tel (323) 651 0902.
sacgla@link2sa.com
New York:
SA Consulate General
333 East 38th St,
New York, NY.
Tel: (212) 213 4880.
South Africa

South Africa
Department of Home Affairs
Subdirectorate: Visas.

Private Bag X114,
Pretoria 0001,
South Africa.
Tel. (012) 314 8911.
www.home-affairs.pwv.gov.za

EMERGENCIES
Police Emergency
Tel: 10111.

Ambulance, Fire, Mountain Rescue,
Poisoning, Air and Sea Rescue
Tel: 10177.

Child Emergency
Tel: 0800 123 321.

In case of difficulties with an emergency
call, Tel: 1022 and ask for the relevant
service.

South Africa is ideally suited to long-distance road travel with an excellent infrastructure

The Thomas Cook Worldwide Customer Promise offers free emergency assistance at any Thomas Cook Network location to travellers who have purchased their travel tickets at a Thomas Cook Network location.

GAY AND LESBIAN
The Gay and Lesbian Equality Project
Tel: (011) 487 3810.
www.equality.org.za

Gay and Lesbian Association of Cape Town, Tourism, Industry and Commerce
Website with extensive links to accommodation, entertainment and other links.
www.galacttic.co.za

Club Travel
Travel agency.
Tel: (021) 487 4218.
www.clubtravel.co.za

SAA is the national carrier and flies between all major centres in the country

Africa Outing
Travel agency.
Tel: (021) 673 7377.
www.africaouting.com

GETTING AROUND
By Air
South African Airways, Kalula.com, Nationwide and other airlines operate domestic services between Johannesburg and major centres. They also fly to selected smaller centres. Several charter and safari operators fly to out-of-the-way places. Fixed-wing aircraft and helicopters can be charted in all major centres.

By Rail
There is an efficient long-distance service connecting major cities. Trains also run to Botswana, Zimbabwe and Mozambique.

Some routes involve overnight travel – services include sleeping berths, private compartments and a dining car. First- and second-class tickets must be booked at least 24 hours in advance. When booking, ask about discounts and special offers.

Overnight trains have dining cars for first- and second-class travel. Cabins are comfortably fitted out with seats that are converted to bunks at night.

Shosholoza Main Line Services is run by **Spoornet**, the national rail system operator. Phone the central booking number in South Africa.
Tel: toll free 086 000 8888.
International calls.
Tel: +27 11 773 8920.

Modern coaches run between many of the major cities

The Thomas Cook Overseas Timetable, published bi-monthly, gives details of many rail, bus and shipping services worldwide, and is a help when planning a rail journey to, from and around South Africa. Available in the UK from some stations, any branch of Thomas Cook, or by phoning 01733 41677; in the USA from SF Travel Publications, 3959 Electric Rd, Suite 155, Roanoke, VA 24018, Tel: 1(800) 322 3834, sales@travelbookstore.com, www.travelbookstore.com

By Bus and Coach

A large number of daily coach services operate on inter-city routes, day or night. Some services also run to Mozambique, Zimbabwe, Namibia and Botswana. Try to book your ticket 24 hours in advance.

Intercape

Reservations and enquiries.
Tel: (021) 380 4444.
www.intercape.co.za

Greyhound

Customer Care (Nationwide).
Tel: 083 915 9000 or (011) 276 8500.
www.greyhound.co.za

Springbok-Atlas

Reservations and enquiries.
Tel: (011) 396 1053.
www.springbokatlas.co.za

Translux
One of the largest operators.
Reservations and enquiries.
Tel: Johannesburg (011) 774 3333,
Cape Town (021) 449 3333 and
Durban (031) 308 8111.
www.translux.co.za

The Baz Bus
Offers backpackers and budget travellers
a service that takes in most of the major
tourist attractions between
Johannesburg, Durban and Cape Town
including the Garden Route. Also to
Swaziland. Flexible packages available.
Tel: (021) 439 2343.
www.bazbus.com

Hitch-hiking
Although hitch-hiking is widespread, as
many South Africans do not own cars,
it is inadvisable for tourists. Be
cautious before giving lifts or accepting
them.

HEALTH
AIDS
As everywhere, be cautious about HIV
infection and take the usual precautions.
AIDS is highly prevalent in African
countries, and South Africa is no
exception. *(see box on p13.)*

Drinking Water
Tap water is purified and is 100 per cent
safe to drink.

Hospitals and Doctors
Doctors are listed in local telephone
directories under 'Medical Practitioners'.
Most large hospitals have efficient
casualty sections open 24 hours a day.

Inoculations
Visitors from most western countries do
not require inoculation certificates. It is
best, however, to seek medical advice if
travelling through other parts of Africa
before visiting South Africa.

Insects – Bites and Stings
In South Africa there are a number of
insects or creatures that cause bites or
stings. Most are relatively minor, but
African bee stings can be quite virulent.
Anti-histamine cream is usually
adequate to ease the pain, but medical
advice may be necessary, especially if the
child has an allergic reaction.
    When visiting game reserves or rural
areas it is a good idea to wear shoes at
night, as scorpions are often out and
about hunting. Some have extremely
toxic venom and, should someone get
stung, medical advice must be sought.
    Blue bottles, which sometimes wash
up on beaches, are small floating
creatures, which can deliver a painful
sting. Lifeguards usually offer assistance,
but medical advice may be necessary.

Malaria and Bilharzia Precautions
Visitors to the Mpumalanga Lowveld,
Limpopo, the Kruger National Park and
the game reserves of KwaZulu-Natal
should take anti-malaria medication as
prescribed by a doctor.
    It is inadvisable to swim in some
rivers and lakes in the eastern and
northern regions of the country, as the
bilharzia parasite may be present.

Snakes
More than 130 species of snake occur in
Southern Africa, but only about 14

species are considered to be dangerous enough to cause death in humans. Most snakes move out of the way of people, and it is extremely unlikely that you will get bitten. (More South Africans die after being struck by lightning than from snake bites.) In the event of a snake bite, it is important to stay calm and get medical advice as soon as possible. Try to remember the colour and size of the snake.

Sunburn

Skin cancer is one of the most common cancers among South Africans. Avoid the most intense hours of sunlight – 11am–3pm – and remember that water provides little protection against ultraviolet (UV) radiation. Always wear a hat. Sun protection measures are essential for young children. Use sunscreen with at least an SPF 15+.

For more information on skin cancer, and the rules of sunbathing, call the Cancer Association of South Africa *(CANSA), Tel: 0800 226 622.*

INSURANCE

Medical treatment must be paid for by the patient. It is wise to take out travel insurance which covers accidents, illness or hospitalisation. Travel insurance policies can be purchased through branches of Thomas Cook and most travel agents.

Drivers insurance can be taken out through car rental companies.
SA Tourmed sells travellers medical insurance that covers the entire Southern Africa region.
Tel: (021) 979 4419.
www.sa-tourmed.com

MAPS

Excellent regional and city maps are available from South African Tourism and regional publicity associations nationwide. Most bookstores have a good range of local maps produced by Mapstudio.

Jacana Media produces some of the best maps and concise guides to the Kruger National Park.

Foreign exchange facilities are available in most major centres

MEDIA

The South African Broadcasting Corporation runs more than 18 radio stations, broadcasting in 13 languages. It also broadcasts three major news and entertainment TV channels and one satellite channel. There are also a number of independent radio stations. Satellite TV with a large choice of international news and entertainment stations is widely available. Thousands of periodicals, journals, newspapers and magazines are published on a regular basis. There are a number of national daily and Sunday papers.

MONEY MATTERS

Currency

The South African currency unit is the Rand, denoted by the symbol R (international symbol ZAR). It is divided into 100 cents (c). Bank notes are issued in denominations of R200, R100, R50, R20 and R10. Coins come in 1c, 2c, 5c (being phased out), 10c, 20c, and 50c; Rl, R2 and R5.

Exchange Facilities

Banks may request identification when changing money. Shop around for cheaper commission rates.

Money Transfers

If you need to transfer money quickly, go to any of the major banks for assistance.

Credit Cards

Most businesses, tour operators, air-lines, hotels and restaurants accept international credit cards including VISA, MasterCard, American Express and Diners Club. Petrol stations don't accept them.

Well-stocked pharmacies are easily accessible in most cities and towns

Thomas Cook

Thomas Cook traveller's cheques free you from the hazards of carrying large amounts of cash and, in the event of loss or theft, can quickly be refunded. South African Rand cheques are recommended, though cheques in all other currencies are acceptable. Many hotels, shops and restaurants in tourist and urban areas will accept traveller's checks.

NATIONAL HOLIDAYS

1st January – New Year's Day
21st March – Human Rights Day
Variable – Good Friday
Variable – Easter Monday
27th April – Freedom Day
1st May – Workers' Day
16th June – Youth Day
9th August – National Women's Day
24th September – Heritage Day
16th December – Day of Reconciliation
25th December – Christmas Day
26th December – Day of Goodwill

OPENING HOURS

Banks are open Mon–Fri 9am–3.30pm & Sat 8.30am–llam. Automated Teller Machines (ATMs) are situated outside most banks and are open 24 hours a day. Shops are usually open Mon–Fri 8am–5pm & Sat 8.30am–1pm. Some stores stay open all Sat & Sun.

PARKS AND RESERVES
National Parks

These are run by the South African National Parks. Most parks in KwaZulu-Natal are run by Ezemvelo KZN Wildlife. The other provinces also run the smaller parks in their areas.

Entrances to parks and reserves close at sunset, but aim to arrive well before that. It is best to do thorough research before booking accommodation to ensure that your wildlife experience meets your expectations. Travel agents will be willing to help or you can visit the following websites.
SA National Parks
www.park-sa.co.za
KZN Wildlife
www.kznwildlife.com
South Africa Tourism
www.southafrica.net
Call Centre. Tel: 083 123 2345.

Regional tourism offices will have details of smaller parks. *(See regional tourism websites on p188)*. Most travel agents and the South African Tourism website have details of private game reserves and lodges.

PHARMACIES

There are numerous pharmacies nationwide and they are easy to find. Should you require medicine after hours, it is best to ask at the hotel or B&B, as very few pharmacies stay open at night. Some private hospitals have pharmacies that are sometimes open later than others.

PLACES OF WORSHIP

Churches of every denomination, synagogues, mosques and Hindu temples are all represented in abundance. Generally, South Africa's population is religiously oriented, and religious beliefs play an important role in public affairs.

A sense of humour is essential in Africa

POLICE

The South African Police Service (SAPS) can be contacted 24 hours a day. (See listing of SA Police Service under Government Departments in local phone directories.)

Many small hotels and B&Bs may also hire the services of private security companies that respond to burglar alarms. Management will give you details if applicable.

POST

Post office hours are Mon–Fri 8.30am–4.30pm, Sat 9am–12am. Letters and parcels can also be mailed via the Postnet chain of stores, which has branches nationwide.

PRICES AND TAX

South African prices have increased considerably over the past few years so it is worth doing some research before booking accommodation and tours. Having said that, petrol is relatively inexpensive, as are local wines and spirits.

VAT, currently at the rate of 14 per cent, is levied on most items and services, including hotel accommodation, goods, transport and tours. You can claim VAT back on goods priced higher than R250 at the airport of departure, various harbours, and customs offices. The original tax invoice, the VAT refund control sheet, your passport and the item are required. Please refer to the VAT shop at the international airport.

PUBLIC TRANSPORT

Public transport in most South African cities is erratic. There are bus services in most of the bigger cities, but they tend to stick to limited routes, run infrequently and close down at night.

Minibus taxis are the most common form of public transport. The standard of driving, however, is usually poor, and the vehicles are often uncomfortable and sometimes unroadworthy.

Cape Town has a reasonably efficient suburban and city rail service. Taxis can be arranged by hotels, restaurants or by looking in the Yellow Pages telephone directory. Ask for a quote before setting off.

SENIOR CITIZENS

Facilities for senior citizens are not comprehensive. In general, expect discounts on cinema and theatre tickets and at some museums. If you feel you should be offered a pensioners' discount it's best to ask.

The Association for Retired Persons and Pensioners

Tel: (021) 531 1768.

Age in Action

Tel: (021) 426 4249.

STUDENT AND YOUTH TRAVEL
Hostelling International South Africa (HISA)

Helps provide student cards, information about discounts and other services.

73 St Georges Mall, 3rd Floor George House. Tel: (021) 442 2251.
www.hisa.org.za

TELEPHONES

South African telephone call charges are expensive, and hotels add a significant charge to your call. Phone cards for public phones can be purchased in supermarkets, at Post Offices and so on. Other public telephones accept coins.

Cellular phones (mobile phones) can be rented at airports and at cellular-phone stores. Most UK cellular phones will work in South Africa. South Africa has an extensive cellular-phone network, and renting a cellular phone is a far more reliable way of

South Africa's telephone system has improved considerably over the last few years

communicating than relying on public telephones.

Dialling codes

South Africa: 27
Cape Town: 021
Durban: 031
Johannesburg: 011
Pretoria: 012

Useful numbers

Directory Enquiries: 1023
International Operator (for booking or placing international calls): 0900
International Directory Enquiries: 0903

THOMAS COOK

The Thomas Cook Network partner in

Minibus taxis are an essential mode of transport for many South Africans

South Africa has a sophisticated and efficient banking system

South Africa is Rennies Travel, with branches throughout the country. Rennies offer foreign exchange, commission-free cashing of traveller's cheques and other services.

Rennies Travel Foreign Exchange
24 hours, nationwide.
Tel: toll free 0861 11 11 77.

TIME

South African Standard Time throughout the year is two hours ahead of Greenwich Mean Time (Universal Standard Time), one hour ahead of Central European Winter Time, seven hours ahead of US Eastern Standard Winter Time and eight hours behind Australian Eastern Standard Time.

TIPPING

A 10 per cent service charge is generally expected in restaurants, not usually included with the bill. Raise the tip to 15 per cent if you have been particularly well treated.

Leave something for hotel staff such as chambermaids. Taxi drivers should receive 5 per cent of the fare on top, and luggage porters R5 per bag.

TOILETS

Most tourist venues, service stations and shopping centres are fairly well served by public lavatories. In nature reserves and national parks, standards of cleanliness are usually fairly high.

TOURIST OFFICES
South Africa
South Africa Tourism
Bonjala House, 90 Protea Rd,
Chiselhurston, Sandton.
Tel: (011) 895 3000.
www.southafrica.net

Overseas
Australia
South African Tourism
Level 1, 117 York St,
Sydney, NSW 2000.

PO Box Q120, QVB NSW 1230.
Tel: +61 2 9261 5000;
fax: +61 2 9261 2000.
blanche@southafricantourism.com.au

France
South African Tourism
61 Rue La Boetie,
75008 Paris.
Tel: +33 1 456 10197;
fax: +33 1 456 10196.
satourism@afriquedusud-tourisme.fr

Germany
South African Tourism
Friedensstr. 6-10,

All major banks are well represented throughout the country

Frankfurt, 60311.
Tel: +49 69 92 91 290;
fax: +49 69 28 0950.
info@southafricantourism.de

Italy
Via Mascheroni,
19 – 5 Floor,
20145 Milano.
Tel: +39 02 4391 1765;
fax: +39 02 4391 1158.
info@turismosudafricano.com

United Kingdom
South African Tourism
6 Alt Grove London SW19 4DZ United
Kingdom.
PO Box 49110,
Wimbledon,
SW19 4XZ.
Tel: +44 (0) 20 8971 9364;
fax: +44 (0) 20 8944 6705.
info@uk.southafrica.net

United States Of America
South African Tourism
500 5th Ave,
20th Floor,
Suite 2040,
New York NY 10110.
Tel: +91 212 730 2929;
fax: +91 212 764 1980.
newyork@southafrica.net

Regional Tourism offices
Eastern Cape Tourism
Tel: (0431) 701 9600.
www.etourism.co.za

Free State Tourism
Tel: (051) 430 8206.
www.fstourism.co.za

Gauteng Tourism
Tel: (011) 327 2000.
www.gauteng.net

KwaZulu-Natal Tourism
Tel: (031) 366 7500.
www.kzn.org

Limpopo Tourism
Tel: (015) 295 8262.
www.limpopotourism.org

Mpumalanga Tourism
Tel: (013) 752 7001.
www.mupumlanga.com
Northern Cape Tourism
Tel: (053) 832 2697.
www.northerncape.org.za

North West Tourism
Tel: (018) 386 1225.
www.tourismnorthwest.co.za

Western Cape Tourism
Tel: (021) 426 4260.
www.capetourism.org

TRAVELLERS WITH DISABILITIES

For information about special needs –
tours accommodating wheelchairs,
services, handbooks and so on:
**National Council for the Physically
Disabled in South Africa**
Tel: (011) 726 8040.
**South African National Council for the
Blind**
Tel: (012) 346 1171.
**South African National Council for the
Deaf**
Tel: (011) 482 1610.

Conversion Table

FROM	TO	MULTIPLY BY
Inches	Centimetres	2.54
Feet	Metres	0.3048
Yards	Metres	0.9144
Miles	Kilometres	1.6090
Acres	Hectares	0.4047
Gallons	Litres	4.5460
Ounces	Grams	28.35
Pounds	Grams	453.6
Pounds	Kilograms	0.4536
Tons	Tonnes	1.0160

To convert back, for example from centimetres
to inches, divide by the number in the third
column.

Men's Suits

SA/UK	36	38	40	42	44	46	48
Rest of Europe	46	48	50	52	54	56	58
USA	36	38	40	42	44	46	48

Dress Sizes

SA/UK		8	10	12	14	16	18
France		36	38	40	42	44	46
Italy		38	40	42	44	46	48
Rest of Europe		34	36	38	40	42	44
USA		6	8	10	12	14	16

Men's Shirts

SA/UK	14	14.5	15	15.5	16	16.5	17
Rest of Europe	36	37	38	39/40	41	42	43
USA	14	14.5	15	15.5	16	16.5	17

Men's Shoes

SA/UK		7	7.5	8.5	9.5	10.5	11
Rest of Europe	41		42	43	44	45	46
USA		8	8.5	9.5	10.5	11.5	12

Women's Shoes

SA/UK	4.5	5	5.5	6	6.5	7
Rest of Europe	38	38	39	39	40	41
USA	6	6.5	7	7.5	8	8.5

Caring for Places we Visit

The Travel Foundation is a UK charity that cares for places we love to visit. You can help us protect the natural environment, traditions and culture – the things that make your visit special. And improve the well-being of local families – spreading the benefit of your visit to those who most need it. All of which can make your holiday experience even better! Most importantly, you can help ensure that there are great places for us all to visit – for generations to come.

What you can do:

- Remove any packaging from items before you go on holiday and recycle if possible.
- Do hire local guides and book locally-run excursions – it will enrich your holiday experience and help support local families.
- Hire a car only if you need to. Using public transport, bicycles and walking are 'environmentally-friendlier' alternatives.
- Respect local culture and traditions. Ensure your dress and behaviour is appropriate for the places you visit. Ask permission before taking photographs of people or their homes.
- Turn down/off heating or air conditioning when not required. Switch off lights and turn the television off rather than leave on standby.

- Do use water sparingly. Take showers instead of baths, and inform staff if you are happy to re-use towels and bed linen rather than replace daily.
- Don't pick flowers and plants or collect pebbles, seashells, coral or starfish. Leave them for others to enjoy.
- Don't buy products made from endangered plants or animals, including hardwoods, ivory, corals, reptiles or turtles. If in doubt – don't buy.
- Do buy locally-made products – shopping in locally-owned outlets and treating yourself to local food and drink is a great way to get into the holiday spirit and also benefits local families.
- Always bargain with humour, and bear in mind that a small cash saving to you could be a significant amount to the seller.
- Coral is extremely fragile. Don't step on it or remove it, and avoid kicking up sand.

For more tips and information on The Travel Foundation and its work, please visit *www.thetravelfoundation.org.uk.*

the
travel foundation
caring for places we love to visit

ACKNOWLEDGEMENTS

Thomas Cook Publishing wishes to thank the following photographers for the photographs reproduced in this book, to whom the copyright in the photographs belong:

Mike Cadman: 1–21, 23, 30, 31, 33, 34–45, 48–59, 61–67, 71, 75, 76, 78, 79, 81, 84, 87, 92–95, 102, 103, 106, 110, 112, 120, 121, 123, 124, 126, 130, 132, 133–137, 140, 142, 143–146, 149, 156, 157, 159, 161, 164, 166–168, 172, 173, 175–177, 179, 181, 182, 184–187
Trevor Samson: 25, 30, 107–109, 111, 113–118, 125, 126, 128, 129, 131, 140, 141, 147, 148, 156–158, 162, 166, 169
All remaining pictures have been credited on the relevant pages.

Travellers

Feedback Form

Please help us improve future editions by taking part in our reader survey. Every returned form will be acknowledged. To show our appreciation we will send you a voucher entitling you to £1 off your next *Travellers* guide or any other Thomas Cook guidebook ordered direct from Thomas Cook Publishing. Just take a few minutes to complete and return this form to us.

We'd also be glad to hear of your comments, updates or recommendations on places we cover or you think that we ought to cover.

1. Which *Travellers* guide did you purchase?

_____

2. Have you purchased other *Travellers* guides in the series?

Yes ☐

No ☐

If Yes, please specify_____

3. Which of the following tempted you into buying your *Travellers* guide: (Please tick as many as appropriate)

The price ☐

The cover ☐

The content ☐

Other_____

4. What do you think of :

a) the cover design? _____

b) the design and layout styles within the book?_____

c) the content _____

5. Please tell us about any features that in your opinion could be changed, improved or added in future editions of the book:

_____

_____

Your age category: ☐ under 21 ☐ 21-30 ☐ 31-40 ☐ 41-50 ☐ 51+

Mr/Mrs/Miss/Ms/Other

Surname_____ Initials_____

Full address: (Please include postal or zip code)_____

_____

Daytime telephone number: _____

Email address: _____

☐ Please tick here if you would be willing to participate in further customer surveys.

☐ Please tick here if you would like to receive information on new titles or special offers from Thomas Cook Publishing (please note we never give your details to third party companies).

Please detach this page and send it to: **The Editor, Travellers, Thomas Cook Publishing, PO Box 227, The Thomas Cook Business Park, Peterborough PE3 8SB, United Kingdom.**

tear along the perforation

The Editor, Travellers
Thomas Cook Publishing
PO Box 227
The Thomas Cook Business Park
Peterborough, PE3 8SB
United Kingdom